WHAT THEY'RE SAYING ABOUT

OVER WHELMED

Jennifer Maggio is a life transformed. She could have resigned to be another statistic. My wife and I are blessed to watch her life now—a display of grace and mercy and the transforming power of Jesus Christ. Hers is a voice that needs to be heard in situations of domestic abuse and violence. *Overwhelmed* offers hope to all who haven't had everything in their life go perfectly. And it will help all of us who want to represent the heart of Jesus Christ to wounded souls.

—Dino Rizzo, lead pastor of Healing Place Church
in Baton Rouge, Louisiana, and author of *Servolution*

Overwhelmed is a journey through immense struggles, personal doubts, and the challenges that face single moms everywhere. Jennifer's empowering story offers hope and clarity that will inspire with every turn of the page.

—Carolyn Gable, radio host and author of
Everything I Know as a CEO, I Learned as a Waitress

You either are one or know one, which makes this book relevant for everyone. Within these pages, you will learn about the trials and struggles of Jennifer Maggio's life and how God lit the way for what is her ministry today. Wherever you are in your life's journey, *Overwhelmed* is a source of encouragement, peace, and strength as it provides practical advice to live out the abundant life God has planned for you.

—Millie Nettles, speaker and author of
I Love You More Than That

If you are seeking a mentor and friend to help you find your joy and peace as a single parent—someone who has been there, done it, and wants to come along side others—read *Overwhelmed* now! It is filled with insights and understanding of the difficulty but also the peace of learning to trust Jesus.

—Beckie Stewart, speaker, women's pastor,
and author at *Mommies Magazine*

Overwhelmed should be required reading for young women across the nation. The hope and practical advice found in this book will challenge and inspire single parents to see past their current situations and dream for something greater. Maggio's experience, both as a parent and businesswoman, has equipped her to speak with authority to a population desperate for answers.

—Donna Frank, speaker and author of *Straight... From Hell*

OVERWHELMED

JENNIFER BARNES MAGGIO

OVER WHELMED

THE LIFE OF A SINGLE MOM

Tate Publishing & Enterprises

Published by Tate Publishing & Enterprises, LLC
127 E. Trade Center Terrace | Mustang, Oklahoma 73064 USA
1.888.361.9473 | www.tatepublishing.com

Tate Publishing is committed to excellence in the publishing industry. The company reflects the philosophy established by the founders, based on Psalm 68:11,
"The Lord gave the word and great was the company of those who published it."

Book design copyright © 2010 by Tate Publishing, LLC. All rights reserved.
Cover design by Leah LeFlore
Interior design by Stephanie Woloszyn

Published in the United States of America

ISBN: 978-1-61663-361-5
1. Biography & Autobiography / Women
2. Family & Relationships / Parenting / Single Parent
10.04.06

DEDICATION

To my husband, Jeff, who stood by me and supported the dream of working with single mothers, even when it did not make sense. You are the light of my life. You are my life partner. I love you.

To my awesome, wonderful children. Much of my life's work has been dedicated to the betterment of your life. You are all my heart, my world. I adore you and cannot wait to see what each of you becomes. I love you.

To my pastors, Dino and Delynn Rizzo, I thank you for allowing me to work with you. Thank you for your leadership in my life and the blessings you have bestowed on my family.

To my twin, who has loved me through thick and thin.

To my countless friends, family, and mentors that have read the book, offered their opinions, and been a listening ear through nights of frustration and stress. Thank you.

TABLE OF CONTENTS

PART ONE: THE STORY

PART TWO: VICTORY IS WON!

PART ONE

THE STORY

PREFACE

As I combed through the shelves of the bookstores, libraries, and pages upon pages of numerous Internet sites, I could hardly find anything on the single parenting experience. There is even less written on single parenting from a Christian perspective. Some will read this book out of curiosity. Perhaps the cover or the title caught your eye. Others will pick it up out of sheer desperation, because you cannot take it another second. The journey is too long and too hard. You are tired. You are looking for help. You might be thinking, "Maybe this chick will have something to say that can help me get through this almost unbearable time in my life."

Some of you married well and had a picture perfect life, but you woke up one morning and it all seemed to vanish. Your whole world fell apart. You go through an ugly divorce and all you have to show for it is alimony and child support.

But there is another group of women out there, single moms who are teenage mothers. There are also moms out there who don't know who the father of their child is. And there are many moms who have not seen their child's father since conception.

There is a passion burning deep within me that I can barely contain; a passion to see every single mom realize that she can make it, that her beginning is not her ending. I want to be real and raw, because that is what a single mom needs.

This is a journey through my life and what I learned about survival, about myself, and most importantly about my heavenly Father. I hope you pick up some tips of survival through these next few pages. I hope you find you are stronger than you thought.

CHAPTER 1

IN THE BEGINNING

My freshmen year of high school was a blast. I spent nine months learning about high school, how to be cool, and who to hang around with. You know, the important stuff. I had finally made it to high school. Isn't that what every kid dreams of, to hang out with the older kids?

At the age of fourteen, there was not one thing you could tell me about life that I didn't already know. I had it all figured out. I was young and carefree. My parents were just plain old and dumb, in my opinion. Besides, they didn't know what it was like to be my age. And I wasn't going to talk to them long enough to explain it.

As I finished up that first year of high school, I could hardly wait for the summer. There would be slumber parties and prank phone calls. There would be no homework and no bedtimes. And there would be boys—new boys, old boys, new crushes, old flames. Oh, the joy of adolescence!

My friends and I hung out almost every day during the summer. We did typical teenage girl things. We sunbathed, read magazines, listened to The New Kids on the Block on the radio, and made fun of our parents. In fact, we made fun of everybody. We giggled and squealed as we told each other silly stories. We called boys, hung up, and called them back again.

We also spent a great deal of time at my friend Jenn's house. There was one major reason for this. She lived in a fairly large neighborhood, much bigger than any of ours. This was important, because it meant more potential to bump into boys. If you don't realize how important that is, then you have forgotten about being fourteen! We would all rush over in the afternoon and spend hours styling our hair and applying makeup. We then went walking up and down every street in the neighborhood laughing, talking, and singing; anything to be noticed. We almost always bumped into boys that we could ignore.

I also enjoyed spending time at Jenn's house because it was always so warm and inviting. Her mom was one of those moms that you could talk to about anything and she wouldn't freak out on you. I found that comforting. Jenn was the friend that made the biggest impression on me in my early years about serving God. She was always at church, always smiling. I do not remember us talking much about church or God in our teenage years, but her actions spoke louder than her words.

There was also our trip to Florida that summer. There is no way the idea of vacationing in Florida, walking along the beach with sand squeezing between your toes, doesn't make you smile. It was the best family vacation I had ever taken. Well … it was the only family vacation I had ever taken. We loaded up late one night in the 1990 Ford Windstar maximum-size van. My twin sister and I were allowed to each take one friend, so the four of us piled into the back of the van and began the thirteen-hour trek. We drove all night and arrived at the beach house at daybreak the next morning. It was breathtaking. My friends and I had never been to Florida. The sky was blue and sea gulls flew through the air effortlessly. The ocean waves were lapping against the shore, louder than I had imagined.

We hurried inside the house to find our bedrooms. It was a two-level ocean-side beach house with all the amenities. It was more than I could have hoped for. We spent the next seven days in paradise. We swam in the ocean, gathered seashells, went on boat tours, and shopped. The days were filled with us riding the waves in-shore on inner tubes and water floats. The waves could be brutal, though. Late one afternoon, I watched as my friend rode a wave that dragged her under several times near the shore. The waves crashed over her head several more times. I became concerned and quickly swam over. I arrived just as she was getting up from this beating, only to catch a glimpse of the water stripping the top of her bikini from her body. She stood, regained her composure, and placed her top back in its proper place as she walked away without a word. It was priceless.

This was the same friend that had gone for a walk earlier that same day and inadvertently fallen into quicksand. She was instantly sucked in waist-deep and began to fight the sand for her legs. After several minutes, she finally won her legs, but lost her shoe in that battle.

The days turned into evenings as we watched the sunset across the water. We would then go get shovels and dig up crabs. There was no particular reason for this, other than watching a furious sand crab scurry from its home and chase us as we ran away screaming in terror. Those were good times. The memories we created during that trip will last a lifetime.

But, by far, the most fun we had that summer were the evening hangouts at the mall. Every Friday and Saturday night, the local mall was the place to be for teens. Now, we did not have permission to go to the mall. I'm not sure why we didn't have permission to go there, other than there would be boys at the mall and they were all standing outside. Yep—outside. They would stare at us as we walked by, and my dad did not like that idea. He did, however, see no problem with us going to the local bowling alley, infested with smoke and forty-year old drunken men with beards and rotten teeth, since it was inside. The logic here escapes me. But this situation presented a dilemma. I mean, all the cool kids were at the mall, so we could not possibly hang out at the bowling alley all night.

The mall was strategically located directly across the highway from the bowling alley. So, we did what any normal fourteen year olds (with a sense of rebellious adventure) would do. After being driven to the bowling alley, we waited thirty seconds for our parents to get out of sight, and we headed across the highway.

We did this several dozen times that summer. It may occur to you at this point that crossing a busy four-lane highway in the dark with traffic going upwards at sixty miles per hour isn't such a good idea. However, we had already discussed it and decided any risk of bodily harm was worth it to get to the mall. I told you I had life figured out. I was practically an adult.

Then, came the fateful day of the accident. We all decided to cross the highway, as we had done many times before. We were running late so we had to hurry. As I approached the median, I ran over the grass, tripped and fell, twisting my ankle on the way down. My friends had already crossed the road. They screamed back at me to hurry. "Get up!" they yelled, not realizing my ankle was twisted. In what seemed like an eternity, although I am certain it was more like ten seconds, I lay in the grass with cars whizzing by at speeds above sixty miles per hour. I screamed, "Go on without me … me … me! I'll be fine … fine … fine!"

As adults, we have laughed many times about how dramatic we were that night. And yes, I did get up and limp over to the mall that night. Summer always lent itself to happy memories for me, like the time my friend slipped on a piece of barbecue chicken, fell down, and her plate knocked her unconscious (Yes, it's the truth!), or the time I busted my shoe open during a friendly game of kickball. I had to wear the ruined shoe the rest of the day while my foot slipped in and out. Summer always allowed me to be in a different place mentally, a happy place. Reality was whatever I wanted it to be. It allowed me to escape, briefly.

That summer I also started a new adventure in my life, high school basketball. I went to my first summer basketball camp. I walked onto the gym floor with a group of kids that I knew were superior to me in athletic skill and ability. But, there I was. I was going for it. After years of prodding from my dad, I walked onto the floor for the first time. I was playing high school basketball. I didn't care much for the sport, actually, but oh, how my daddy did! He loved basketball. I would listen to him talk about his glory days when he was leading point guard of his high school and had been offered basketball scholarships around the state. And so began my basketball career on that hot summer day.

There were forty or so boys and girls in the gym. The whistle blew and we ran, and ran, and ran. We did dribbling drills, lay ups, free throws, and jump shots. And we ran and ran and then, ran some more. The whole thing lasted about three hours. It was a blur. I did throw up, which any good athlete will tell you is a good thing. I was dizzy and near fainting, I'm sure. My face was beet-red and sweaty. My long ponytail flopped and stuck to my sweaty face as I practically crawled to the water fountain outside the gym. I was a joke when it came to playing basketball.

I noticed a tall boy standing with a group of other kids waiting in line to get water, too. I knew him from school. Well, that's to say, I knew his name. He was a basketball player for our high school team. We had had some classes together through junior high school. I knew him as a class clown. However, today, he looked kind of different, kind of cool, and kind of cute.

My turn came up at the water fountain. I couldn't help but notice that he watched me as I walked away. *This could get interesting,* I thought to myself, as I walked away trying to be as attractive as possible with a red sweaty face. I began to wonder if he had a girlfriend and what he was like. I knew he was a great athlete, as anyone could tell, but what else was there to know about this guy? Maybe I would just have to find out.

Welcome to my first day of basketball camp!

I come from a very traditional Mississippi family (if you can call the story I'm about to tell you traditional). By "traditional," I mean racist. Let me be clear in saying that I am not in any way insinuating that every Mississippi family operates under these same set of rules, or even that my own family still does, for that matter! But in 1935, when my dad was born, there was a clear line with black and white relationships. I paused to mention this for only one reason. The tall basketball player I mentioned was quite literally tall, dark, and handsome. He was black.

I completed that long week of basketball camp, running and sweating all the while. The boy and I innocently flirted throughout the week, tossing each other quick glances or smiles, or conveniently getting into the same drill lines. I found myself thinking of him throughout the week. Of course, I thought about quite a few boys that summer. I mean, I was fourteen, after all.

I didn't see the boy for the rest of the summer. I went on with my summer plans, visiting relatives, swimming with friends, sleepovers, the whole nine. In fact, I didn't think about him again until several months later.

In August 1992, I began my sophomore year of high school. Oh, the anticipation of a new school year. You lie awake at night thinking of the first day of school. How will my teachers be? Will the classes be hard? Will my friends be in my class? Will there be any new boys at the school? I began classes that hot August day, and there he was, basketball boy. We did have classes together. We began to talk a little at a time. We would share notes or smile. We then moved on to sitting together at basketball games. There's something exciting about young love, about the newness of a new relationship. What began as innocent flirting turned into a full-blown romance that year.

However, the seven years that followed were anything but romantic…

CHAPTER 2

CHILDHOOD

When I was three years old, I awoke late one night to some type of commotion in the kitchen. With my favorite blanket in tow, I stumbled down the hall, half-asleep. I was horrified to see my dad leaning over the kitchen sink while my step mom and sister-in-law leaned over him washing blood from his head and face. I stood there shocked as they cried and scrubbed him clean. At some point, I was noticed and quickly ushered back to bed. I didn't know what to think of all this. I lay in bed that night scared and confused. I cried myself to sleep wondering what had happened to my daddy. I later learned that my dad had driven his 1978 Chevrolet Silverado into a large ravine that night, yet somehow managed to get it out and drive home. The windshield was crushed. The truck was dented. My step mom stitched his head at home to avoid questioning from authorities. He was driving drunk. This was the earliest memory of my dad. In those early years, it was rare that I saw him without a Miller Little Pony (beer) in his hand.

My daddy was raised an honest, hard-working farmer in a family with six children. His parents married at fifteen years old. They raised chickens and pigs and grew their own vegetables. They worked from sun-up to sun-down. My daddy really did miss the first few weeks of school every year due to picking cotton! His mother made all of his clothes by hand and washed them with a washboard. They didn't have electricity and used coal oil lanterns for many years for lighting at night. They had no indoor plumbing and, therefore, used an outhouse. Many years after indoor plumbing was installed, I remember my grandmother still using the outhouse. Old habits die hard, I guess.

Growing up, my dad's family churned their own butter. They killed and cooked their own pigs. They hunted deer and turkey and fished at the local ponds. Trips to town were rare and only made when absolutely necessary. Times were hard. My dad was raised on country music and gospel hymns by a tobacco-chewing daddy and a thick-skinned Mississippi momma. It was simple living. He grew up in the fields working and playing until dark. He eventually grew to love basketball and became quite good at it. He worked hard with his grades and was offered basketball scholarships to go to college after his high school graduation, but he chose the United States Army instead. He spent a couple years in the army and later married his high school sweetheart. They raised two sons together, but they divorced after almost twenty years of marriage. Both of his sons were born with heart problems. One had major surgery as a young man, and the other had a heart-related condition.

My dad knew this son was dying and lay awake at night and watched his son's heart beat up and down in his chest, fearing that any night would be his last. I cannot imagine what this does to a parent, to watch their child die before their eyes, but my brother did die after a long battle with his heart. This crushed my dad emotionally, and he turned to drinking to solve his problems. This was not to say that he didn't drink prior to this event, but he was a full-scale alcoholic by the time I was born. He had also been a very active deacon in the church, but he completely fell away from any activity associated with the church after his son died.

My daddy already had a lifetime of disappointments before I was ever born; a failed marriage, the death of his son, the death of his baby brother a few years prior, and disappointments through his local church, and I do not believe he ever fully recovered from them.

My dad met and married my mother a few years later. I was born shortly after in 1977, along with a twin sister, in a rural Mississippi town, not far from where my dad was raised. I do not know much about my parent's relationship, other than my daddy's drinking interfered with it. I know that my dad was violent with her, and that my mom was unhappy. Their relationship was a roller coaster of extreme emotions, either ultimate bliss or utter turmoil. My mom was exhausted from it all. She eventually began to turn her heart back toward the things of God, where she had found comfort in her childhood. She actively attended church with my sister and me. She began to play the piano for the local church and would lend her angelic voice on occasion. She longed for my dad to be part of her church family, but the hurt from his past kept him blinded.

One Sunday in November 1978, my daddy had gone deer hunting, as he did most every weekend during hunting season. There was lots more beer drinking than hunting going on during these trips. My mother got us dressed as usual and rushed out the door for church. She loaded us in our car seats and we began the short trek . Our church was less than five miles down the road. Out of nowhere, a teenage drunk driver slammed us into a tree, less than a mile from our own home. My mother was killed instantly. My dad heard on the radio that there was an accident with fatalities on the street where we lived. He knew that his wife had been killed. My sister and I suffered major bruising, cuts, and scarring. We were unable to walk for months after the event. Neighbors, friends, and family rallied around to help care for us as my daddy dealt with his grief.

The shock of my mother's death hit the whole family hard. The young, beautiful Sammye was gone. What would happen to her twin babies? Her whole life had been ahead of her. She was but thirty-two years old. We had family from all over the country arrive for her funeral. There were plenty of pictures taken that night to put in an album for us when we were old enough to understand. I looked through that photo album many times growing up, wondering how my life would have been different with my mother living.

It seemed that almost by daybreak my dad had remarried again, wife number three was named Barbara. My dad worked offshore as a drill man for an oil company, which meant that he worked away from home a week at a time. I remember a conversation that I had with my dad years later about his third marriage. He confessed to me that he married Barbara as a babysitter for us, as he still needed to provide a living for us after my mom was gone. I remember very little about Barbara. I do, however, remember that her form of punishment was to lock us in a closet for extended periods of time. When Daddy was away at work, she would not feed us regularly. She beat us for disobeying, even at two years old. As quickly as she came, she was gone. I do not know why.

In my family, there was kind of a code of silence. No one was asking my dad why he felt the need to marry over and over again. No one dealt with the alcoholism. Whether it was through shame or some sick loyalty, I cannot say. All that is for certain is in a world of double names like Nannie Lou, Mary Alice, and Louisa Mae, you knew that someone would knock you in the head if you aired too much dirty laundry. That's just the way things were in those days. All my southern country girls know what I'm talking about. There is something about a wide-waisted Mississippi woman in an apron with a wet dishtowel that you just don't mess with. You learn to accept your world as normal.

When daddy married wife number four, we were pretty used to the idea of our home being a revolving door with people coming and going regularly. We called each wife "Momma," as we were told to do, and didn't speak of our own mother very often. Our new Momma, Francis, came with a teenage son, John. By the time I was three years old, my stepbrother was molesting me while he allowed onlookers to watch. We never discussed any of this. It would be many years before I learned that this sort of thing was not normal and many years after that before I ever discussed it aloud.

Daddy and "Momma" would go out to dinner and leave us under the supervision of the neighbors next door. They had an older son, Jamey, who also molested me. We would be sent next door to play with him many, many times through those next few years. As a child, I cannot tell you exactly how I felt about all of this. I have only been able to remember bits and pieces of that period in my life. I remember more bad than good, unfortunately. My dad was gone quite a bit with work. We were left in the care of Francis most of the time.

There were later problems in this marriage, too. Infidelity was involved. I was brought to my dad's friends homes, all of which were women, to stay the night. We stayed up watching rated R movies at four years old, while they visited in the bedroom.

Momma Francis had her own problems. She rolled marijuana and smoked it regularly with her friends in front of me. She had some extra-curricular activities of her own, not the least of which was sleeping with someone in our own home that I walked in on, while my dad was at work. They divorced shortly thereafter.

As I said earlier, my dad had a drinking problem. This coupled with a bad temper and multiple divorces led to some rocky nights in my home. He would come home drunk and tear up the whole house, destroying lamps, pictures, chairs, and anything else in his way. He screamed violently for hours on end. He would cry and kick chairs. He would hit on the different women in his life. He drove home drunk many times, including straight through our front yard. He made large circles over and over again with his truck on our lawn, honking and screaming, all the while. To a young girl looking out the window to see your front yard torn up with a speeding vehicle is terrifying.

My dad was an angry drunk. When he consumed alcohol, he became mean and violent. Anyone who wronged him would hear about it in his drunken frenzies. This was no different the night he stood at the end of our driveway with pistol in hand as he screamed obscenities at my uncle across the street. My uncle, in turn, stood at the end of his driveway screaming back with his pistol in tow. This standoff lasted for some time as I watched through my bedroom window, fearing my daddy would be killed. Most of the time he didn't remember any of it the next morning, and we all acted like it never happened. By the time wife number five came around, he drank until he passed out regularly.

There was never a period of more than a few weeks when a woman didn't live in our home. So it was no surprise when Candy showed up, wife number five. That is when the adventure really began. My dad adored her. She was twenty years his junior. She had three children of her own, which made a total of five children in our home, all roughly the same age. He stayed married to Candy four years.

During those four years, I was between nine and twelve years old. Many events ran together. My dad changed jobs several times, but always stayed away from home working for extended periods of time. This left us home alone with Candy. In her youth, Candy had gone through some brushes with the law and was on probation most of their marriage. Her own children had been living with their grandparents. When she married my dad, she took on five children and was learning how to raise us effectively. She failed miserably. There was something deeply disturbing about her parenting style. She was very child-like and oftentimes treated us like her mental equivalents and not her children.

Candy had an eight-year-old son who was mentally handicapped. When she married my dad, her son had been living in a special facility for the mentally impaired. We retrieved him from the facility soon after they married. Candy was in no way prepared for the responsibility of caring for him, so the burden was carried by us all. We were too young to have such a task, but we did it. We four girls, aged nine to eleven, took turns feeding him, changing his dirty diapers, and often bathing him. I was not bitter about having this task, but I now look back and think it was inappropriate for pre-adolescent girls to constantly view and clean genitalia of a same-aged boy. In addition, the responsibility of caring for a mentally-challenged individual should be left to parents and professionals, not little girls.

There were many things that were inappropriate about Candy's parenting. I was only ten years old when she first brought pornography into our home. She had stolen the videos from a local video store. She began playing those in front of us. At such a young age, I was infiltrated with thoughts and images that no child should experience. I remember her laughing quite vividly as we hid our faces in shame. Theft, dishonesty, pornography, and infidelity were all part of this relationship. As children, she would drive us around at night, and we would be asked to steal newspapers from the yards of neighbors rather than get our own subscription. We would take yard art from the yards. She wrote insufficient checks all over town. She even stole my dead mother's wedding ring from a picture album and pawned it for money. We were officially white trash.

Candy would do many childish things. As a joke, she would chase us around the house with a cup that was filled with her own feces. She would sit on us and restrain us, while spitting in our faces. She was an obese woman. I can remember her sitting on top of me topless while she slapped me in the face over and over with her very large breasts as she laughed hysterically. She beat me with the belt many times. She slapped me in the face many times. She screamed that she hated me and threatened to throw hot gravy in my face once. She slammed me against the wall and choked me until I felt I was going to die. She wasn't really going to kill me. She wanted to bully me. She loved us one day and hated us the next. One day, she would sneak around behind my dad's back and let boys come over to our house and other days we would get beaten for a boy even calling us. There was no consistency.

One of the other normalcy's of the time was to spend the night with Candy's parents, our step-grandparents. They would let us play outside for hours after dark on the trampoline and prepare us our favorite meal for dinner, macaroni and cheese. They hugged us and doted on us. They let us take turns driving the riding lawn mower. They did all the things grandparents were supposed to do. At night, we took turns sleeping with grandma and grandpa, because they slept in separate beds. Grandpa began inappropriate behavior with me almost immediately. I never told a living soul. I was scared Candy wouldn't believe me or that I would tell my daddy and then he would go back to work leaving me alone with Candy and that she would beat me.

Through all that, I loved her. She was my mom for that short while. I had no mother. I wanted so desperately to be loved. There were normal times during all the turmoil, where we went to church as a family and had Sunday dinner afterwards. We had big family Thanksgivings and Christmases with extended family. We had large family gatherings that would last for hours. The adults visited inside the house, while all the children played until dark outside. I cherished those times. I needed that normalcy, even if it was only pretend and only temporary.

CHAPTER 3

AND SO IT GOES

I nfidelity crept into my dad's marriage to Candy also. They soon divorced. Through the years my dad had many girlfriends and wives. At this point, you may be questioning why he did some of the things he did. Why did he make some of the decisions he did? Why didn't he protect me better? Don't. It's a fruitless thought-process that won't bring you any closer to the answers than I am today. All I know is that when people are hurting, they do strange things. I know that when Jesus isn't the center of your life, a series of bad mistakes will mount on your shoulders like the weight of a thousand years. I let go of wondering "Why?" a long time ago.

The divorce from Candy was very ugly. There was lots of fighting over money, who was going to get the bedroom furniture, the pots and pans, the end table. Everything was an argument. Physical fights occurred at my house when Candy would arrive in a fury about something regarding the divorce.

In the days leading up to the divorce, Daddy loaded us in the car at night and we drove around looking for Candy to see what she was up to, driving from bar to bar until the wee hours of the morning. Candy did the same to Daddy. The whole thing seemed to drag on forever. The day the divorce was official, I was so relieved that I would never live with her again. Yet, in some way, I was sad; sad that yet another mother was gone.

Not long after Candy left, at only twelve years old, I began feeling pressure to have sex. Part of the pressure was that I hung around with people much older than I was at the time. The other part was pressure I put on myself because I wanted to be liked and to fit in with the cool kids. We spent many hours on the weekends driving around aimlessly from one teen hangout to another. We drank alcohol most every weekend. I remember a friend getting alcohol poisoning and nearly dying, but it didn't matter. She was out drinking the next weekend and so was I. My dad never noticed that I came home drunk, repeatedly. The episodes had gotten so bad that there were times I couldn't remember anything about the night before. Daddy was preoccupied with his own life and dating.

I put off the pressure of having sex until I was thirteen.

I had avoided it as long as I could, and since I was dating a sixteen-year-old, I just did it. We drove several miles in the middle of nowhere and it happened. That night in a field in no man's land, I thought so little of myself that I gave away one of the most precious gifts my heavenly Father gave me. It was over in a matter of minutes and I felt sick. I knew he didn't love me. What had I done? I didn't tell anyone, but it wasn't long before my entire circle of friends and his friends knew. I was embarrassed and ashamed. The guy barely spoke to me afterwards.

My dad was oblivious to my new lifestyle. I jumped from one short relationship to another, each with a similar story, only to have my heart broken over and over again. The guys didn't call me afterwards. Most of them were many years older than me. Oftentimes, I just became another face in the crowd, another notch on someone's belt.

The next eighteen months of my life were that way. I battled back and forth with what I was doing. I wasn't happy. I wanted to stop this cycle of emotional turmoil, but I couldn't. It saddens me to even think upon those things now. I was so lost, lonely, and hurting. I needed someone to love me. There was so much abandonment in my past. As soon as one boy would show me attention, I latched onto it. Half of the time, I didn't even feel bad about it. I almost thought of it as survival, a means of masking how I really felt. I felt the call of God on my life, on the one hand. On the other hand, I felt certain that he didn't know what my life was like. He didn't know the things I had to endure. Certainly, no one in that church knew of the things that went on behind closed doors at my house.

You see, I had been attending church all my life. My daddy didn't usually attend with us. He would drive up to the front door, drop us off, and leave. I felt embarrassed when I saw normal families all sitting together. I thought my family was weird, and I was pretty sure everyone else did, too.

One Sunday, after the pastor spoke on sin and its consequences in your life, I walked down to the front of the church during an invitation the pastor gave to come change your life and get right with God. I was nine years old during that time. I had asked Jesus to come into my heart. I was so excited and full of joy. I began to read my Bible daily and prayed regularly. I was baptized the following Sunday. My dad went to church that Sunday, and my grandparents even drove in from Texas. It was a big day. The next couple of years, I became very close with God. Until age eleven, I attended church three times weekly. Even with all the abuse I suffered, I still committed to being at church.

I made several good church friends. I did enjoy hanging out with their families. It gave me a sense of belonging. There was something great about being with genuinely good girls that came from good families that loved the Lord. It was peaceful and they always made me feel welcome.

But slowly, I began to slip away from those friends and the church. The distractions from home were too much. My stepmom made fun of me for being a goody-two-shoe who thought I was better than everyone else. Her behavior, along with my newfound interest in boys, made me put the Lord on the back burner. That's where I kept him for many years thereafter. And that's where I found myself, away from God, entering one lonely relationship after another.

During this same time, my dad had been dating around

a bit. He began to date a sweet woman from the area, whom he later asked to move in with us. He had dated her years earlier and reconnected with her through friends. She had a lovely personality and was the closest thing I had had to a real mother in a long while. I loved her instantly. She was an excellent cook and had begun teaching me some cooking techniques. She adored my dad. That was evident. Although he had not drunk in several years, Daddy slowly started having a beer on occasion. Before long, he progressed to drinking heavy liquor again.

One afternoon, Daddy disappeared for several hours. His girlfriend made phone calls and drove around looking for him. He finally arrived home, and to no one's surprise, he was drunk. He screamed about this and that, stumbled around the house, and eventually passed out. The following day, he kicked out the sweet woman I had grown to love with no warning. My twin sister and I were devastated (as was the woman), but we had no say in Daddy's lady decisions.

Within fourteen days, we met Mary. Mary was in her forties with bleached blond hair. She wore heavy blue eye make-up and long artificial fingernails. She reminded me a great deal of Tammy Faye Baker in appearance. Although she smiled and spoke kindly to me, there was something about her that made me very uncomfortable. One of the first things she told me after we met was that she wanted to be friends and hoped I would learn to confide in her. I believed her for about thirty seconds.

Two months later, she became wife number six. She and Daddy were married in a small ceremony at our home with a small gathering of friends and family present. My friends and I sang at their wedding. We decorated their car for their honeymoon. We threw rice on them as they jumped in the car and drove away. I wondered, as I waved, how long this one would last. I can't say that I cared one way or another.

Mary was the first wife since my own mother's death that I did not call "Momma." I was fourteen by now and had had just about enough of all that. My attitude reflected as much, too. Mary had three adult children that had been raised by her ex-husband, so she had very little parenting experience. From day one, I emphatically believe that she resented that my dad had twin teenage daughters still living at home. She hoped we would disappear, and when we didn't, it became her mission to hate us. She was very successful at it.

At first, things seemed fairly normal, whatever that means. Daddy and Mary did their own thing as newlyweds. They went to dinner and watched movies. They visited with friends. My dad had a very strict persona, in that boys weren't allowed to call our home or come over. But the truth is, I had very little supervision and I took full advantage of it. I ran from one thing to another. I had sleepovers with whomever I wished. I sneaked out of the house. I sneaked boys over after dark.

Is it any wonder that at thirteen years old, I began to have sex?

In this desperate need to be loved, I was Miss Perfectionist. I was the classic over-achiever. I was a straight A student. I was class president. I was a member of the Library Club, the Fellowship of Christian Athletes, and the Beta Club. I was on the homecoming court and in Sweetheart Pageants. I was a peer counselor. I was the one chosen to give all the speeches and opening prayers at school assemblies. I was the most intelligent on the school basketball team. I was given the Spirit Award. Any honor that I could have possibly won, I fought hard to win it. At least in that moment, I was on top of the world. I felt respected. I felt loved.

It seemed that no matter how hard I worked, it was never good enough, though. I had teachers, coaches, and counselors that encouraged me through the years, but not my dad. And I even think my dad bragged about me to friends and family, but he rarely told me that he was proud of me. He never gave me a big hug and told me to never settle for less than God's best. He didn't tell me I was a princess that was waiting on just the right prince. Sure, we hugged if I went out of town or something. But there was never just a spontaneous I-love-you hug.

I can even remember my high school baccalaureate service. My twin sister and I had been announced Co-Valedictorians of our graduating class only days before the service. It happened to be held on the Sunday morning of Mother's Day. As a tribute to mothers, our school decided to have each graduate's mother sit with them during the service. At some point in the ceremony, we would hand a red rose to our mother. Because our biological mother was deceased, it was expected that my stepmother would accompany us to the event. However, she did not, nor did my dad. So as not to sit alone, we had two kind teachers to volunteer to sit with us.

I can remember my embarrassment as if it were yesterday. I had obtained the highest honor bestowed upon a graduating senior, and still, it was not good enough. I was hurt and humiliated. Daddy was a man's man who was raised to not express much emotion. It was not masculine.

I consequently grew up with very little affection. I loved my dad more than I can express. For nineteen years, he and my twin sister were the only two constants in my life. No matter how many mistakes I made, he was still my dad. I loved him, but I just couldn't talk to him. I sat beside him on our front porch in silence dozens of times through my teenage years. I wanted to talk to him so desperately. A thousand thoughts roamed through my mind, questions I wanted to ask, but I couldn't. I just couldn't.

His current wife was no better. Mary had expressed her desire to get to know my sister and me in the first few weeks of the marriage. Those feelings soon dissipated, and she became what I later referred to as "the evil step-mother." From all the stepmoms we had, I thought she was the most abusive. All the other's abuses were blatant, out there in plain view. But Mary's abuse was much more secretive and calculating.

Not any one incident made her abusive. It was the culmination of many events. My dad worked away from home, so again, we were left with a stepmother to watch after my sister and me. She didn't treat us the same when Daddy was around as when he was gone. When he was away, she would stop by a restaurant on the way home from work and pick up dinner only for herself. She brought it in, went to her bedroom, locked the door, and ate it. When she did this, we began to cook dinner in the kitchen. She would then come from her room screaming at us for mess-ing up the dishes. This was a frequent occurrence. When our dad was home, however, she bought enough for the whole family.

She also bought new clothes for herself three to four times weekly. Never did she buy anything for us, not even a shirt. However, we were required to wash all her clothes separate from the rest of the family, "Because your clothes will mess up my clothes," she would say. She bought a few things for Daddy from time to time, but she pretended we did not exist.

Unbeknown to my dad, she ultimately began recording all phone conversations coming into and out of our home. She recorded each call and later listened to them. Why? Had I gotten involved with drugs? Was I engaged in some illegal activity? No. This was a way to control and manipulate us. She would recite some of the things I said to my friends in front of the family or sneer about feelings I had expressed to girlfriends. The phone recordings went on for two years.

Like every wife before, she came into the family insisting we went to church on Sundays. We did this for a brief time, until I would mess up. If I was disobedient in any way, she began to scream that I wasn't a Christian and the whole church thing was a farce that she wasn't going to participate in anymore. She once made me sit down with the pastor, a man I barely knew, for counseling. Why wouldn't my own parents sit down and talk to me? Couldn't my dad see that I was hurting?

There were moments in my junior high and high school years that were genuinely happy. I did a great job of masking all the ugly underneath. I enjoyed the spotlight. I enjoyed my Daddy giving me a big hug and telling me he was proud of me, however rare that moment was. I liked that people thought I was smart. I would absorb any compliment given to me and hang on its every word.

By the time Mr. Basketball Boy came along at the end of my freshman year, I was ready for any compliments thrown my way. And compliments he had! This dreamy, talk, dark, and handsome basketball player was as smooth as silk and said exactly what I wanted to hear. Dillon played for the varsity high school basketball team and all the girls liked him. He was a star athlete. When he began to show me some attention, it didn't take long for me to latch on. It didn't matter that he had a girlfriend. It didn't matter that he was black and I knew my dad was not going to like that. In fact, it made it better! It was something unachievable that I could conquer.

We sat together at basketball games and talked on the phone after school. We spent hours on the phone learning every detail of each other's lives over the next several months. By the middle of basketball season of my sophomore year, I was sneaking Dillon into my house. We spent many nights together that next three years. In the beginning, we were very discreet about anyone even knowing about our relationship for fear that my dad would find out. I didn't tell my friends. I only told my sister. Part of me was scared of what my friends might think, and the other part was terrified about what my dad would do.

But the biggest part of me didn't care what anyone thought. I was going for it.

CHAPTER 4

THE RELATIONSHIP

Eventually, my dad did find out about the relationship. It was ugly. One night, Dillon and I had decided that he would come over to my house and spend some time, as he had done many times before. My sister and dad had gone to the local high school football game. I chose to stay home. Dillon came over at around eight o'clock that night. I pretended to go to sleep because my stepmom, Mary, was home. She came in the other end of the house and walked in the bedroom. I was so surprised to see her that I began to fumble my words. She immediately caught on that something was wrong. She saw Dillon lying on the floor on the other side of the bed. I was horrified. I had been caught. I was no longer Daddy's perfect princess. Mary called my dad at the game that night. They called the cops. I didn't want to disappoint my dad, but I wasn't sorry. I loved Dillon. I almost instantly began to think about how I would continue to see him. We would just have to be more creative.

It seems that that incident only made it more exciting to sneak him over. It only fueled my passion and love for him. I was totally in love. He was so handsome, so cool. I began to not care who knew of our relationship. I told my friends one by one. The news traveled through the school like wildfire. Little Miss Perfect finally had a flaw. Many friends were no longer my friends because they disapproved of me liking someone who was black. I began to feel more isolated.

Did I mention that Dillon had a girlfriend? Yep. He hung with her most days at school, holding hands and pretending everything was okay. I just walked around and pretended not to notice. I convinced myself that the only reason he wasn't with me was because our parents didn't want us together. In fact, I created this whole Romeo & Juliet love story that made me think that all our troubles related to how the world and our families didn't want us together. But once we were adults … once we were adults, we would be together forever. He loved me, too, ya know.

I continued this same story in my mind as he began to get more and more and more girlfriends in the year that followed. He had broken up with that original girlfriend, but he still wasn't acknowledging our relationship to anyone, although he spent most nights at my house. By the end of our junior year of high school, I had heard of more girlfriends than I even wanted to count. He slept with numerous girls, even my friends. I began to be so hurt, so broken. Yet, there was that part of me that needed him to love me, to hold me. I needed to hear the words that he told me. "You are beautiful." "You are the one I really love." "You are the one I cannot wait to see every day," he would say. I believed every word.

Before I knew it, I had spent three years in a relationship that was so volatile that none of my friends even wanted to hear the stories anymore. I had gotten so wrapped up in the drama of arguing with other girls, screaming at Dillon, and terrible phone calls that I did not even care that the principal and all the teachers knew about it. My reputation was ruined. And it didn't matter. As long as Dillon and I were together, everything would be just fine.

My sophomore, junior, and senior high school years were filled with these dramatic events that all related to Dillon. When I heard of a new relationship that he was pursuing or a new girlfriend he liked, I would become enraged. *How dare she like him! She knows we are together. She is just trying to mess things up for me. She is just jealous of what we have,* I thought.

I almost always directed my anger toward the other girls, not him. I slapped the girls. I screamed and argued and cussed. I started fights. I wound up in the principal's office more than once. I was in the streets fighting over him with absolutely no dignity whatsoever. I went into hysterics every time I heard the stories. Yet, I still let him come over almost every night. He convinced me time and time again that the rumors were all lies. He constantly told me that he would never love anyone more than me. We would one day be married and live happily ever after. By the time he left my house at night, I was on cloud nine, convinced of his undying love for me, until the cycle started all over again the next day.

I finally graduated high school in 1995. There were approximately four hundred students at the school the year I graduated. There were almost seventy girls pregnant. That's right. It was an epidemic. It was cool to be pregnant. Through my four years of high school, I watched girls one by one become pregnant. I started thinking of what it would be like to have a baby. Would that make Dillon love me even more? Would he leave everyone else so that we could finally start a family? I did not care whether or not I got pregnant. I went on to have two miscarriages before I graduated high school. I hid that very well. My dad never knew. By my senior year of high school, I got pregnant a third time. When I graduated high school, I was named Co-Valedictorian with my twin sister. It was such a proud day to walk across the stage with my twin sister to accept the numerous awards and scholarships.

We both gave valedictory addresses. We received several full-paid scholarships to college. I received more awards that night than I could carry and had to have help loading them in the car after the ceremony. I had everything going for me. Yet, it was such a sad day. I knew I wouldn't be going on to college. I knew I had a baby growing inside of me. And at seventeen years old, I had no idea what I was going to do.

That night after graduation, I went to Dillon's house. I knew this was the last night I would see him for quite some time, and I needed to spend some time with him. My dad had sold our home, and we were loaded up and moving to another state in the morning. Needless to say, Dillon was not near as sentimental as I was. I cried a great deal that night wondering what my future held, when I would see Dillon again. I moved the next morning and didn't talk to him again for several weeks. I did call his home a few times, but he was out of town and no one gave me information on where he was.

The original plan was to graduate high school, move the next morning, and start college a few months later. However, I asked my dad if I could go visit friends for a few weeks back in our old hometown before college started. I packed my things and hugged my dad tightly, fearing this would be the last time I ever saw him. I was six months pregnant by now, although no one knew. Friends came to pick me up, and we headed back to our hometown, our graduation site.

Although my dad thought I was gone for only a few days, I knew I would never return home. After getting settled at my friend's home, I went to the local free health unit to get my first prenatal care. I began the tedious process of applying for government assistance programs—food stamps, welfare, Medicaid, and government housing. At the end of the two-week visit, I had successfully applied for and was receiving all my assistance, but I still had nowhere to live.

I finally told my dad that I was pregnant. I called him and nervously explained my situation. I cringed and waited for his response. His exact words to me were, "Have a nice life." He kicked me out of my house. My twin sister went away to college. I had no clothes, no money, no way to provide for my child, nowhere to live, and no plan.

Dillon finally came home from out of town. We talked and visited over the next few weeks, but he was more worried about going away to college than my well-being. He talked of playing basketball (because he had earned an athletic scholarship) at his new school. I knew that he was not worried about where I would live or how I would survive, but deep down, I needed him. He was all I had left.

One of my closest friends, Jenn, finally invited me to move in with her and her family (the Chapmans). I was seven months pregnant at the time. My generous aunt in Texas had bought a 1984 Mercury Lynx to help me out. That thing left me on the side of the road at least twice per week and smoked so bad that no one could drive behind me, but I was thankful nonetheless. I spent the night in that car sometimes, partly because I felt I had nowhere to go and partly because I didn't want anyone to know how bad I was hurting.

Becky Chapman, Jenn's mom, and her family allowed me to stay with them as long as I needed to. She was the backbone of that family. She cared for me during those next few months as if I was her own child. She became my mom. She was such a special part of my life during that time. Years later, I continued to buy her Mother's Day gifts. She took me to doctor's appointments. She bought me clothes. She spent hours and hours talking to me. She was my comfort in those many lonely months that followed. I will always be eternally grateful that she took me in, provided me meals and a place to sleep. She tried to make me feel part of her family, but the truth is, I was hurting deep inside, missing my own family. I missed my daddy, the one that had been the only constant in my life for so many years. I missed my twin sister that I had grown up with.

That summer, as Dillon was preparing to go away to college, I had begun to hear rumors of another girlfriend being pregnant. I was devastated. Here I was thinking that we would build a family together and that we could finally be together, since we were both adults [?] yes, but he had other plans. I found out that the rumors were true. He did, in fact, have another baby on the way. I felt like the laughing stock of town. I could barely make myself get out of bed in the mornings. In fact, many times I didn't. I began to contemplate giving my baby up for adoption. I didn't know what to do. I was as alone in the world as I had ever been.

It was about eight o'clock one night when the phone rang. It was a long-time friend from high school on the other end. She said, "Jennifer, did you hear that Dillon was getting married tomorrow?" *What? What was she talking about?* I had seen Dillon earlier that day (because he had not left for college, yet) and had no idea. I began to make phone calls and could not believe my ears! Yes, he was getting married in only a few short hours! *How could this be? I don't understand. How could he do this to me?*

I talked to him on the phone much of that night and through the next morning as he got ready for his own wedding. He claimed that he was being forced to do it, because the girl that was pregnant was so young and her parents were forcing him to marry her. I wanted so desperately to believe that. I convinced myself it was true. I can honestly say that even now that was the darkest hour of my life.

At the very moment that he was marrying someone else across town, I curled into a ball onto the floor and cried and cried. I screamed out in terrible pain and torment. I could not stop screaming. I was on my knees screaming, "Why? Why? Why?" It was the closest I have ever been to suicide. I did not care what my future held. I did not care about my baby. All I knew was that my life was over. I did not want to go on. I could not face the world knowing of the shame and embarrassment I felt. I could not handle one more phone call asking how I was taking the news. I could not bear one more report of them leaving on their honeymoon. It made me sick. I cried. I hurt. The pain was almost unbearable. I felt that I physically could not get out of the bed.

I spent the remainder of my pregnancy moping around. I thought many times of giving my baby up for adoption and killing myself. What reason was there to go on? My family was gone. My friends were mostly gone. I had no money, no future. The one person I had been living for had just married someone else. I had never known pain like that before.

As the next few months passed, Dillon went on to college. He called me and wrote me regularly. He told me how much he really loved only me, how this whole thing was a formality and not a true testament of his love to the other girl. I began to slowly have hope again that we may still be together. I hung on every word he said. I lived my life waiting on the phone calls he would sporadically make or the letters he would mail. It was what got me through the last few months of my pregnancy. I decided against giving my baby up for adoption. I just couldn't do it. I knew he would be my ticket to have Dillon in my life.

On November 10, 1995, I gave birth to my precious son. He was almost nine pounds. I spent almost twenty hours in labor. I was surrounded with my new family, the Chapmans, and many high school friends. There were at least ten people in the delivery room that night. I had never seen a biracial baby before, so I did not know what to expect him to look like. He was the most beautiful thing I had ever seen in my life. He was so big, so handsome. I would never let him go. When everyone went home that night, I lay awake. Alone in the hospital, I began to cry. I wondered how I would ever provide for this child. What would I do? What was my plan? I looked at how beautiful he was and knew he deserved way more than I could ever give him.

I cried for most of the year that followed. I went through the motions of life, caring for my son, but I was not really living. I was merely functioning.

Dillon came home from college two weeks after the birth to see our son for the first time. I just knew that once he saw him he would want to quit college, come home, and be the dad that our son so desperately deserved. I know this will shock you, but that never happened. Sure, he held him and commented on how handsome he was. But that was the most he ever offered to our son, a few visits and kind words. After the first time Dillon saw our son, I knew that I had to make plans for our future. Dillon was never going to be there for us. In fact, I had heard that his other child had been born only a few weeks after my own. My mind began turning. I had a child to raise.

Within two weeks, I got my first job. I worked as a waitress for Pizza Hut. I left my son when he was but ten days old to begin working. I did not have the luxury to rest and recuperate. I got a government-subsidized apartment. I was still receiving my government assistances. I moved into my new apartment with no furniture, and people slowly donated one piece at a time.

I was making it. I didn't know how, but I was. I was able to get a television and eventually saved up to get cable! I got a phone. I had enough to buy diapers for my baby. I started college at night at the local community college. I made straight A's for the next two years. I am still grateful to how the Chapman family helped me with babysitting while I began to get my life on track.

My sister eventually married a man from our hometown and moved back home, so she helped me with babysitting also. She helped me with everything! She gave me money to help get my car fixed, to pay my light bill. I eventually moved my baby boy to another in-home daycare facility with my friend, Rhonda. She had operated a daycare for more than twenty years and was well known in the community. She was truly a godsend. She loved my son with all her heart. She cared for him like her own. Many nights, when I would come to pick him up, she would have already fed him dinner and would then offer me a plate. She did not know that I had no food in my pantry. If she would not have fed me so many nights, I would have gone hungry. I am so grateful for her generosity. She became one of my closest friends.

I continued my relationship with Dillon. We talked on the phone and wrote letters several times a week while he was away. He had divorced the other girl, although I later found out that he was still pursuing a relationship with her, as well. I was holding onto that relationship in hopes that he would one day change. I needed him to help me. I needed him to love me. For once ... if I could just have him to love me, we could make our family whole. I became pregnant again while he was home on his college break. I secretly hoped that this second child would convince him to be solely with me. I can remember calling to tell him as soon as I found out. He was back at school, and his response was, "Yeah, I figured that."

Depression came over me again. How could I tell any of my family or friends that I had done this again? I thought of abortion. I knew it was wrong, deep down, I knew. Yet, it seemed like a viable option for about two days. I didn't have the money and I knew I would not get any money from Dillon. And what's more, I knew I could not live with such an act for the rest of my life. Of course, I had lived with so many other acts; I am not sure what made that one so different! Thank God I decided against it.

My son was now one-year-old. I had left Pizza Hut and secured a job as office manager of a local furniture store. I didn't make much money, but it was a nine-to-five-job in a professional environment. I continued to go to college full-time at night, while I worked forty hours a week during the day. I left my son at daycare at eight o'clock in the morning and didn't see him again until ten o'clock that night. I picked him up, put him in bed, and collapsed, all to start again the next morning.

I hid the pregnancy of my second child for five months. I was only nineteen years old and was pregnant for the fourth time. How had my life gotten so far off track? I dropped out of college. There was no way I could continue to go to school and raise two children while working full-time. I continued working at the furniture store. I went into labor on June 27, 1997. I was in labor with my twin sister and my "mother," Becky Chapman, there to give support. I gave birth to a beautiful baby girl. She was breathtaking, I must admit. She had lots of curly black hair and pretty tanned skin. She had big brown eyes and a round face. She was chubby and beautiful. She, too, was almost nine pounds.

I gave birth to her on a Friday. I went back to work on Monday morning. I had no choice. It broke my heart to leave my newborn so soon. I had no maternity leave, no sick leave. I had no other way of paying my bills, other than to suck it up and press on. I worked hard. Bosses like it when you work hard. I found favor with my boss, and he gave me a week's vacation later that same month so that I could enjoy my precious little one. He respected my hard work and determination.

Dillon came home from college to see our daughter only a few days after she was born. He held her and commented on how beautiful she was, just as he had with our son. But there was no gift, no diapers, and no assistance of any kind. In fact, he mostly complained about how hard college was and how he did not have that much spending money, when all the other students did. All the years my children were in diapers and using baby formula, Dillon never purchased them one item. Nothing. Nada. Some way I convinced myself that he was the pitiful one, all alone in school with no money, so in addition to everything else, I sent him care packages and money on a regular basis. Any time I got income tax refunds, I sent him money.

He was back and forth away from college during the next two years. He went to school some nine hours away from home. He would come home a few weeks at a time during the summer, but leave shortly thereafter, anything to stay away from his responsibilities. He called, wrote letters, and visited. One night, very late, I received a phone call. The voice on the other end was crying. She began to say, "You don't know me, but Dillon does. And I'm pregnant." The words rang through the night like a bad dream. I held the phone, unable to speak. I felt myself gasping for air. I could not understand how he could do this to me. I could not see how he would have yet another child after not caring for the ones he currently had. I finished that brief conversation in disbelief. Within a few weeks of this call, I received word that yet another baby was on the way. This totaled five children for Dillon.

He graduated college a few months later. When I finally saw him, there was an immediate argument. "Get out of my life. Get out my house. Stay away from me and these kids!" I screamed. I began to cry and become hysterical. I could not take another second. I could not hurt any more. I could not take another phone call in the middle of the night. He wrapped his arms around me and began to profess his love to me once again. He claimed that the rumors were all lies. He claimed that those girls were lying. I wanted so desperately to believe him. I wanted for him to keep his arms wrapped around me for the rest of my life. I wanted him to stay with only me. He spent the night that night. He was gone by morning.

Over and over and over again through the next several years, I would let him stay the night, and he would always leave early the next day so that no one saw his car at my house. He disappeared for days on end. He would have no explanation when he returned as to where he had been. I became used to the routine of not knowing where my boyfriend was. I even got used to the endless phone calls that came all hours of the day and night looking for him, or to have some young girl proclaim her love for him and how he wanted to be with her. I remember countless nights of crying and screaming. There was the low self-esteem, the depression. What was wrong with me? Why didn't he love me? What was I doing wrong?

I became so blinded by this infatuation that it never occurred to me to be angry at him for not helping to support his kids. Why didn't he get a job and sacrifice the ways I had? Why was I giving him money? I would do whatever it took for him to be with me. I would storm into his other girlfriend's houses or fight with them. I would make phone calls over and over looking for him around town. I loaded my children into the car at midnight and rode around looking for him while they slept. For what? So that I could see that yes, his car was at some other girl's house?

There were many instances of violence throughout my relationship with Dillon. I learned quickly that there would be consequences if I didn't just mind my p's and q's. That's not to say that there weren't times when I didn't just start the argument anyway, because I definitely did.

I was fifteen years old the first time that Dillon became abusive with me. We were sitting in my bedroom. I had a conversation with him about how I was talking at school to a friend of mine, who happened to be a boy. He told me that he didn't like when I talked to other boys. It made him uncomfortable. He ran his hands through my long hair and then grabbed me by the hair tightly. His demeanor instantly changed. He whispered in my ear that he did not like it and that he didn't want me talking to this boy again. Very quietly, I said, "Okay," unsure of what had just happened. I now find it ironic that he was so threatened by my other conversations with boys that he would be violent with me, but he, on the other hand, could talk to, kiss, or sleep with any girl he wanted.

I was only a few months pregnant with our second child when the next incident occurred. I had been visiting at his parent's home and had come outside to leave. I noticed a car sitting nearby and recognized it as an old girlfriend of his. I began to question him about it and was furious by his nonchalant response, I became angry and hysterical. He kept telling me to calm down and the more he did, the louder I got. Before I knew what was happening, he had grabbed my hair and began banging my head against the rear view mirror of his truck. I was so shaken up that I walked away crying and delusional. A few weeks later, just after the birth of our second child, I found him with another girl and flagged him down on the side of the road. He was so angry that I was confronting him that he grabbed my hair and banged my head against the steering wheel over and over, as I sat in my car, with our children. He then threw my keys out the window into a ditch and drove off. How had I fallen into this trap?

Through the seven-year-relationship, there were many instances similar to the above-mentioned. He pulled my hair, choked me, and shoved me around. He would tear up my house, throwing things about the room, breaking them. He would scream and push me. He bloodied my ear. He threw me to the ground and restrained me many times. I fought back often and had bruises all over me to show it. I never shared with one friend of his violence because I was embarrassed about it and even more embarrassed that I continued to take it. I could not bear for others to know one more thing that would add to the volatility of this relationship. I tiptoed around arguments with him to avoid a confrontation. When he cheated on me, I pretended not to notice or care.

I wasn't the only one he was violent with. Incidents came up through the years where he attacked other girls. At one point, he was arrested and jailed for his abuse. He had broken into a girl's home that he had had a relationship with. She was severely beaten with bruises and bulging blood vessels to prove it, but she later dropped the charges.

As time went on, it was more of the same. I continued to work extremely hard to make ends meet, which barely happened, while Dillon floated from one thing to the next. He rarely worked and had begun to smoke and sell marijuana. He jumped from one girl to another and one job to another. There continued to be episodes of violence, emotional abuse, and drug abuse in our home. Our children also continued to grow as Dillon missed more and more birthday parties and Christmases. He never provided one pair of shoes, one diaper, or one meal for our children in those years.

I am enlightened of the insanity of this situation now, but at that time, it seemed that Dillon was all I had. I know I didn't truly have him either, but I convinced myself that I did. After seven years in the same situation, I wondered if it would ever end. When would enough be enough? For some of you reading, you cannot imagine taking that many years of abuse or enduring the dozens of instances of infidelity. But for those of you who have endured this same vicious cycle, you understand completely. I pray that the former group will never know this kind of pain.

In those same years, I resumed a relationship with my

dad. He moved back to our hometown, where I was living, with his sixth wife, Mary. Daddy had been a smoker for more than fifty years, and it had finally caught up with him. He was dying of cancer. I watched my dad form a relationship with my children like none other . He adored my kids. He invited them to visit with him at his home, took them driving on Sunday afternoons, and bought them little trinkets. He had stopped drinking a few years prior and seemed to mellow out in his old age.

He knew I had pursued a relationship with Dillon against his better judgment and it angered him, but we rarely talked about it. We didn't talk about the past at all, as was par for the course. In those last years of my dad's life, I watched him rededicate his life to the Lord. He dragged his oxygen tank behind him and walked with a cane, but he went to church. He made efforts to call me regularly, and we visited each other often. It seemed that facing his own mortality had significantly increased the importance of knowing his grandchildren.

All I had wanted for so many years was my daddy's love. I saw my dad become more gentle, kind, and loving as he held my children. The last months erased a lifetime of hurt in my life. I was able to release bitterness and anger that I had carried for so long. I sat on his bed one afternoon and held his hand. With fear in my heart and a shaky voice, I asked my dad if he was a Christian, if he knew the Lord as his Savior. He said that he knew without a doubt that he was going to heaven and that he was a Christian. Even though I was not living my life fully for God, I took great comfort in hearing those words.

Within a week of that conversation, my daddy was dead. Cancer had eaten away at his entire body. I was twenty-three years old. The grief that overcame me was like someone letting all the oxygen out of the room. The grief was literally suffocating. I needed to be held, to be comforted. My twin sister had her husband with her, but I had no one. I felt the weight of the world on my shoulders. Now, both my parents were dead.

I stood at the funeral alone, surrounded by friends, yet still alone. The one person that I needed to be there for me wasn't. My kids needed their dad and I needed my boyfriend, but he was never there to console me. As the weeks passed, Dillon never said he was sorry about my dad's death. He barely acknowledged it. He never put his arms around me so that I could just cry.

From that moment on, I knew that this season of my life was changing. I didn't know how or why, but I knew my life would never be the same.

CHAPTER 5

HOW DID I WIND UP HERE?

I t is important for me to talk about my emotional state at this point in my life. I do not think you can effectively understand my decisions until you understand the devastation and hurt I was feeling.

We have all read the headlines of children killing their parents or serial killers stalking dozens of people. We have even heard of children on rampages with guns at school shootings. It is hard for us to wrap our minds around such violence and tragedy. All of those things are shocking and we begin to question why people would do such things. Let me assure you that this insanity didn't happen overnight. With the exception of legitimate mental illnesses, many of the individuals in those incidents had a slow deterioration of their self-esteem, their self-worth. That's exactly what happened to me. While I didn't go on to kill someone, I certainly was slowly dying inside.

My self-esteem disappeared. It was a slow process. I did not see it happen, but one day it was gone. Growing up, I was told often how pretty I was. Family and friends commented on my beauty. I competed in pageants. I was fearless and self-confident. I would sing and dance for family and friends. I was always up for performing a speech or a song. I always felt pretty. I always felt smart. Through my early adolescent years, I felt like I could accomplish anything. Yes, I had suffered great pain in my life. But, overall, I still felt like I held the world in the palm of my hand. I could be anything I wanted.

When Dillon first entered my life, the one thing that stands out above all else is his endless compliments. If I heard it once, I heard a thousand times how beautiful I was. He told me how pretty my eyes were. He brushed my long, brown hair and told me how he loved it. He complimented my figure. He told me how smart I was and how proud he was of me when I would walk across the stage to accept an award at school. I remember one instance where he had walked up to me in the early part of the tenth grade. I looked down to get some papers from a notebook. When I looked up, he just stared at me and said, "God, you are so beautiful!" It is funny that even now, fifteen years later, I can still remember that exact day and how it made me feel.

As this relationship progressed, I began to seek that validation more and more. It mattered what he thought of me. The very course of my day could be determined by whether or not he complimented me or if I caught him talking to another girl that day. It began to determine my self-worth. As with many relationships, the longer we were together, the fewer compliments I received. However, my need for them did not diminish. Because I wasn't getting any validation at home, Dillon became more and more important to me.

Through the years, he became more critical of me. If I wore a shirt or jeans and he said he did not like the way it looked, then I never wore it again. If he said I needed to cut my hair in a particular style, I did. If he said I needed to keep this kind of toothpaste or that kind of cereal in the house, I did. I remember spending hours on my hands and knees scrubbing the kitchen floor on the eve of his arrival home from college, so it would be perfectly clean for him. This was not because he had asked me to, but because I wanted everything to be perfect, free of error, so that he wouldn't want to leave my apartment and go to someone else's apartment. If I saw him showing interest in another girl, I secretly tried to dress like her or wear my hair in a similar fashion. Anything I could do to make myself or my surroundings more appealing to him, I did.

With the arrival of new girlfriends in his life, this process became an obsession. In the years we were together, Dillon pursued dozens of other relationships. Each time he did, I would vow never to speak to him again. With his great persistence, I always gave in. And thus, the cycle would continue. I questioned in my own mind what might be wrong with me. I must not be pretty enough or thin enough. The house isn't clean enough. Everything that could possibly be wrong, I tried to fix. I dieted to lose weight, and then he would say I was too thin. So, then I would eat to gain weight. All of this was an attempt at pleasing him. As you can probably suspect, it never was enough. It never deterred him from doing anything he wanted to do. And I wound up miserable.

By the time Dillon married another woman, my self-esteem was already so low that I didn't think it could get much worse. I was wrong. I had suffered rejection after rejection in this relationship, and countless others before this one, but this was the ultimate blow. To hear that a man you love has chosen someone else to marry and not even told you is beyond comprehension, especially when you spent years deriving your self-worth from him.

As I mentioned earlier, the news of his marriage was so unexpected that I didn't know how to cope. I was eighteen years old at the time. Upon hearing the news, I curled onto the floor in a ball and screamed uncontrollably. I wailed and cried for hours until there were no more tears to shed. My reaction was so severe that my friends discussed hospitalizing me for fear I would lose the baby. I wandered around for weeks afterwards, hopeless.

Within a few months, I had given birth to my son and post-postpartum depression set in. I suffered with depression for over a year. I had lost everything—my family, friends, boyfriend, and my future. I spent my children's toddler years barely functioning. My happiness solely depended on whether Dillon was around. As time passed, he would be in and out of the picture, away at school, then at home again, living with me, and then living with someone else. If he was around and treating me well, then life was grand. Otherwise, I was going through the motions of life.

To add to this depression, my financial situation was dire. Making ends meet was a stretch. I had to calculate down to the penny the gas for my car, rent, and food. There were no extra trips to the grocery store, because I didn't have the gas or the food money to do it. There was no extra money for clothes, so I depended on donations or store credit. For Christmas, we had toys donated to us, and I wrapped them and re-gifted them to the children. I can count on one hand the number of times my children got new clothes in the first several years of their lives. I received an annual Christmas bonus of $50 on Christmas Eve every year that I worked at the furniture store, and I rushed out to buy the kids a new toy each, and pay for our Christmas meal. The kids and I ate alone many Christmases and Thanksgivings, as we patiently waited for Dillon to come around, usually late that evening, after he had visited his own family and his other children.

The shame I carried was almost unbearable. I was embarrassed about my finances. I was embarrassed that my boyfriend had children from one state to another. I carried shame about my past sexual abuse and guilt about my own sexual immorality. I couldn't go back to church because I did not feel good enough to be there. I couldn't tell my friends and family the details of my situation because I knew they would wonder why I had endured the abuses for so long. It all seemed hopeless.

In addition to the financial and relationship struggles, I was hit in the face with blatant racism. As I said earlier, I had never seen a biracial child when I gave birth to my son. That is how uncommon interracial dating in my area was at that time. It was not just that long-term friends avoided or ignored me. It was the constant glares from patrons at restaurants or the rude gestures. It was dealing with the lies that were constantly spread about me around town . My son was called a racial slur at four years old by a fellow preschooler. I even had a stranger come up to me in a local shopping mall and say, "Get out of here and take that little black baby with you." It was horrible and it further alienated me from people.

As the shame and embarrassment was mounting in my own life, my dad had struggles of his own. As I watched him slowly die of cancer, it changed me. I had been as strong as I could for as long as I could. I had been caring for my children alone, working countless hours, because I knew no one else would do it. I stayed up late nights washing clothes and changing bed sheets. I was alone at the hospital when my daughter was hospitalized with pneumonia, when the ambulance came as she vomited blood at two years old. I did all the late-night feedings demanded by infant children. I put myself through school. All of those things were tough, but watching my dad die was by far the toughest. For all of his mistakes, he was still my dad.

His death was the pivotal moment in my life when I knew things would never be the same again. When I watched them lower him into the ground, it was like some of me was buried with him, the bad parts. The shame, embarrassment, and the hurt were all being buried. I knew I had to move on to something new.

CHAPTER 6

A NEW DAY

Several things changed in the twelve months surrounding my dad's death. At the constant urging of my twin sister, I finally visited her church. I had lived my life so far from the things of God that I felt sure He would strike me with lightning as soon as I entered the building. I would like to say that I had a life-changing experience that day at church, but I didn't. I did, however, attend again, and then, again. Before long, I was going three times a week, just as I had as a child.

My life did not change instantly, but I began to find more comfort in church than I ever had. I felt the pastor speaking directly to me in the services and it moved me. It was changing me. I dedicated my free time to volunteering. Any time the church doors opened, I was there.

One Sunday, the pastor spoke on tithing. Giving ten percent of my income to the church was not a new concept for me. I had heard this biblical principle while growing up and attending church. The problem was that I had no extra money. As the months went by, I could not get this idea of tithing off my mind. I finally decided to just do it no matter how much money I had. I started giving ten percent of my income faithfully every Sunday.

I had been working at the same furniture store for five years. The company was unable to provide me with benefits or much of a pay raise. There was little opportunity for growth, so I began to search for a new job. I had been happy at the furniture store, and it was definitely my comfort zone by now, but if I was ever going to get off food stamps and welfare, I had to look for something else. I found a job making twice as much money and put in my two weeks notice. The job fell through unexpectedly, and I was left with no job. Since my current job had already found my replacement, the owner of the furniture store helped me secure a new job with a large financial institution.

I had no idea what a blessing I had walked into. When I accepted the job, I thought I would be making $22,000 per year. This was far more than the $9,000 per year I was currently making, but still barely enough to stay off food stamps. I was still happy with the increased income and newfound benefits, such as medical and dental insurance, childcare, and a 401k retirement plan. I learned my new business quickly. Little did I know, the position I accepted not only had a higher salary, but also provided earning potential from commissions. It is not by accident that I landed this job six months after I began tithing. The day I began tithing, a bill never went unpaid in my home. The money just seemed to always be there.

I proved to be very good, and sales and commission came easy. I went from making $9,000 a year to six figures annually. The new job afforded me travel opportunities for training and prizes or vacation packages for successful sales months. I went from never leaving my small hometown to traveling extensively, dining in fine restaurants, and becoming debt-free. It seemed the more I gave to the Lord, the more financial freedom I experienced.

Although I was beginning to be financially free, I continued to struggle in other areas of my life. I was continuing the relationship with Dillon and wrestled with permanently leaving him. I continued to sleep with him, but as I became more active in the church, I was more convicted. By the time of my dad's death, I was in an all-out internal war. As much as I loved Dillon, I knew he would never change and I needed a new start. I decided to leave Dillon for good, and I moved to a new town a couple of hours away from him.

As I moved into this new season of my life, I knew there would be hard times. I knew things would be different. I would be lying to tell you that I never saw Dillon again. I did invite him to my new home several times, but each time, I knew God was changing me. I did continue to have sex with him sporadically. And each time I did, I felt enormous shame and conviction. I knew I wanted to be closer to God, and Dillon created a barrier. I believe now that God filled me with a new desire in my heart. I believe he filled me with a strength that I had not had before. My heart became hardened towards Dillon, and over that next twelve months, I began to see myself without him. I knew I could make it.

There was still an almost unbearable loneliness within me. I wanted to have someone. My kids and I had spent too many holidays alone. I prayed for years that God would somehow make Dillon the one for me, that God would change his heart and turn his life around. I prayed God would show him the error of his ways and make him love me. I was in church on a Sunday morning and was praying that same prayer, even though Dillon and I were no longer together. I secretly still wanted that big, happy family. I began to feel something very vividly in my heart. I can remember that feeling like it was yesterday. It was God telling me not to pray for changes for Dillon, but pray for changes for me. *Begin to pray that you will change, Jennifer.* I believe that day that I did change. I stopped praying for God to send me a godly husband. I began to accept that I was not going to be married, and I was okay with that.

In fact, I was more than okay with the idea of not being married. I began to embrace my singleness. I was overcome with a sense of peace that everything was going to be okay. I had been at the lowest of lows in my life. I had a new attitude. I felt different. I began to feel like I did not need a man to love me. I could make it on my own. I began to feel freedom in the idea that my past was my past and God had set forth a new day for me. I was totally at peace with God being the father of my children (in the sense that he was our provider), and I lost the obsession to make their earthly father behave differently.

As I mentioned earlier, I had moved to a new town a couple hours away. I transferred with my company. I walked into the office the first day and was introduced to the staff. One gentleman caught my eye, for no other reason than he was handsome. As the months passed, I began to spend more time with my co-workers. I loved my job so much. The Lord was blessing me immensely, and I was making more money than I had dreamed I could. In fact, I was making more money than anyone in my family had ever made. I no longer had financial struggles. I no longer felt burdened by my past mistakes. I slowly began to think of this new co-worker as more than a friend.

Jeff was a nice guy. He was a Christian that was active in his local church. He had pretty green eyes with salt and pepper hair. He was just about my age. He had broad shoulders and a nice smile. He was a hard worker, who had become very successful with our company. He did not have any children of his own. When I allowed my mind to stray for a moment, I immediately convinced myself that Jeff would never be interested in me. How could he be? I had so much abuse in my past. I had two children outside of marriage. I was not a good enough Christian. Why would someone who loved the Lord, had a great job, and had no kids want to be burdened with my baggage? Jeff and I went out with groups of friends on occasion. As time passed, I finally got the courage to call him and tell him my true feelings.

Jeff felt the same way, and we began dating. We talked on the phone until the early hours of the morning. We took the kids out to dinner. We had dinner at my house and watched movies. It was so exciting. We soon began attending church together. He was great with the kids. I was promoted with our company a few months later and moved away. We continued dating long-distance. Some time later, he transferred with the company to be near the kids and me. He later asked me to marry him. I couldn't believe it. We had won a trip to San Antonio and were taking a gondola ride on the river through the middle of the city. That evening, we stood on a balcony overlooking the city, and Jeff told me he wanted to spend the rest of his life with me. I was elated. I called everyone I knew and immediately went into planning mode.

We married in early spring of the following year. The wedding weekend was full of the usual hustle and bustle that such an event brings. There were bridesmaids and guests I had not seen in ages arriving from out of town. I was full of emotions, as my bridesmaids and I stayed up most of the night talking and giggling on the eve of my wedding. Then, the day arrived.

We all got up early and rushed around town with last-minute preparations. We had manicures and pedicures. We all had our hair and makeup professionally done. I was receiving dozens of phone calls from those who couldn't come. Friends and family helped to get my children dressed as I began the task of climbing into a forty-pound wedding gown. It was a beautiful halter-style floor-length gown with a sweetheart neckline, pearl and sequined beading along the bodice, and a five-foot train. I wore a diamond tiara with a lace wedding veil.

It was an outdoor event of the grandest kind. Jeff and I worked hard in the prior months to pay for every penny, and we did. It was far more than I could have imagined.

We were married at a Victorian mansion in the middle of New Orleans, the most romantic city in the region. Most of our family and friends were present. The wedding march began to play. I watched as long-time friends marched down the aisle, and I was beaming. But when my children, my little girl in her flower girl dress and my little boy in his tuxedo, held hands and began the journey toward the front of the altar, I lost it. I stood there with tears streaming down my face and a floodgate of emotions overwhelmed me. All the hurt, pain, and disappointments of the past had now been replaced with joy and thanksgiving in my heart.

We finished the ceremony and danced the night away. All too soon our Rolls Royce limo pulled up to take us to our honeymoon destination. I kissed the kids and hugged friends goodbye. And as we drove away, I knew I was embarking on a new journey, a new life with a wonderful husband. The Lord had finally given me the desires of my heart.

We bought a new home and settled in New Orleans for some years. The home was twice the size of anything I had ever lived in. We stayed faithful to church. Our careers flourished. The children were happy and thriving. We vacationed all over the country. My heart was full and I was finally free.

A few years later, Jeff adopted my two children. He is now their legal father. He loves them just as if they were his own. And what's more … they love him, too. They are happy and healthy with tremendous athletic and academic abilities. They have grown into a beautiful young man and woman who volunteer with local missions and are active in our church.

In January 2007, we welcomed home our latest bundle of joy, a beautiful baby girl. Our family is now complete. As I look back over the years of heartache and loneliness, I know that it was merely a season, a short period of time. It was a learning period in my life.

Am I saying that there have not been hard times since I have married Jeff or since I have found Christ in my life? No. I could write another book on the struggles that we have gone through. Here's the difference. I have a new hope that surpasses all understanding. I know that no matter what this life brings I am ready. I am armed and prepared. I have a husband that thinks I hung the moon. Now, even eight years later, he tells me daily that I am beautiful. He tells me of what I mean in his life. He puts the Lord before all others. My heart is full of joy.

PART TWO

VICTORY IS WON!

CHAPTER 7

OVERCOMING ABUSE

Abuse comes in all forms; sexual, physical, emotional, and verbal. Every form of abuse is detrimental to your overall well-being. I want to say that again. Every form of abuse hurts. Oftentimes, we make light of emotional and verbal abuse, as if those were less important or less impactful than the others. The truth is, many people can move past the physical beatings much more quickly than they can the words that accompanied them. Have you ever seen a forty-year-old woman say that she can still remember her father telling her that she wasn't pretty? We tend to hang on to verbal abuse for years. The Bible says in James 3:6 that, "...the tongue is a flame of fire. It is a whole world of wickedness, corrupting your entire body. It can set your whole world on fire..." How true.

The home we grow up in is our litmus test on normal. If we heard daily that we were obese, ignorant, or unintelligent, then that is what we assume is true. If profanity is used in the household regularly, we soon begin to use it without thinking of it as rude or inappropriate. We become conditioned to accept our environment and usually duplicate it later in life.

Growing up, I was never encouraged to talk about my feelings. If I was hurt or angry or sad and began to cry, I was just sent to my room until I could straighten up my attitude. If I brought up anything that made my dad uncomfortable to discuss, then the subject was changed or there was simply no response. All too often, this is true for many homes. Parents do not encourage their children to discuss their emotions, usually because they had their own emotions stifled as a child, or perhaps parents do not know exactly how to respond, so they avoid it. Either way, the consequences are dire.

Even if everything else was fairly normal in the home, the lack of emotional support and verbal affirmation will soon rear its head as a young woman begins to date. We will discuss parenting in Chapter Ten, but this fact is why it is crucial as parents that we are equipping our children for emotional well-being.

As young women begin dating, they begin to look for what they are comfortable with. If they are used to their dad screaming at them or their mom using profanity constantly, then it will not seem out of the ordinary when they find it in a boyfriend. Our high schools are plagued with abusive relationships. Many young women do not even know they are in such a relationship until it has escalated to the point of fear that they cannot get out of it. It may start with an occasional comment, such as, "You sure acted stupid today at school," or "I hate when you wear your hair that way. It makes you look silly." Months or years of hearing these types of comments degrade a young woman, and she begins to lose her self-worth.

Emotional abuse can accompany the verbal abuse or be a different issue altogether. Because adolescent girls are naturally more emotional during the years of puberty, it is expected that there will be what they deem dramatic events in their youth. Boyfriend break-ups are common for the age. However, emotional abuse creeps in when Little Johnny breaks up with her over and over again as an emotional tactic to increase her dependency on him. "I like you today, but I don't like you tomorrow." If a young girl has given herself sexually in this relationship, then the situation escalates. Because teenagers are not prepared for a sexual relationship, young girls can emotionally fall apart when the relationship does not work out. Infidelity can creep into the relationship. The boyfriend will use her and dump her, and then eventually wants her back again. This scenario repeats itself in our high schools and colleges across the country. Our young women are so distraught from suffering with emotional and verbal abuse that by the time they reach adulthood, they do not know how to function in a normal, healthy relationship. Their whole view on relationships is tainted.

This does not stop with adolescence. It is amazing the number of women I counsel that have endured years of abuse as a child or teenager and then find themselves in an abusive adult relationship. She wakes up to a man that she married who has devalued her for years, or dated the same boyfriend for years, and he does the same thing. What's worse is seeing her jump from one abusive relationship to another because she doesn't feel she deserves more.

It is the same for physical and sexual abuse. Many people make comments such as, "Why won't she just leave him? Why does she continue to take it over and over again? Can't she figure out that he is going to do this to her again?" These are clearly the comments of someone who has never experienced abuse or has not been properly educated about abuse. If a woman entered a relationship with little self-esteem (perhaps stemming from childhood abuse), or if her esteem has already been drained through her current relationship, then she does not believe she can do better or even deserves better. If her very existence and self-worth was derived from the man she is with, then when he becomes abusive, she convinces herself that she cannot leave him because she needs him.

As with the other forms of abuse, physical abuse starts slowly. For me, I had my hair pulled at fifteen years old. It was not enough to hurt me, but it scared me. I later thought that he only did that because he loved me and was hurt that I had talked to another boy. He wouldn't do that again. I was sure that I had overreacted. That made the second and third offenses easier to get through. Before I knew it, being pushed or shoved or having my hair pulled was just part of a typical Saturday night.

It breaks my heart each time I work with a young

girl and her story of abuse unfolds. She tells me how he didn't mean to do it and he will not do it again. She makes excuses by explaining what she did that made him so angry. It is never long before I see the same girl come back with bruises on her arms or a black eye and I immediately know. I just know.

As abuse victims, we get so wrapped up in the emotions of the relationship that we cannot see straight. We need our spouse/boyfriend to love us. We need him to give us value. We do not understand why he is doing what he is doing, but maybe if we just talk less or if we try not to upset him, then he will stop. "If I wasn't so annoying, then maybe he would not do this anymore," we tell ourselves. The attachment becomes so great that the longer we are in the relationship, the harder it is to visualize ourselves without him.

Sexual abuse is such a delicate subject. Because of the immense shame surrounding such abuse, many women never confess these victimizations. The most recent statistics supports at least 25% of all women have been sexually abused. Those are the ones who have reported it. Rape and molestation are the most common forms of abuse. Inappropriate touching and/or unsolicited sexual conversations, such as with a minor, are also considered abuse. Exposure to pornography is also a common form of sexual abuse. Many instances of childhood sexual abuse is usually not violent, therefore children are not sure what just happened. All they know is that they do not feel right about the episode, but they are sometimes not sure whether or not to tell someone. In adult relationships, many women have been raped by their boyfriend or husband and do not consider it abuse. They simply feel that if they are in a relationship with him, then his sexual advances are required, even if she refuses them.

It is hard to pinpoint which form of abuse damaged me the most, but I can tell you that viewing pornography as a child ranks highly on the list. For years, I had no idea that it was considered abuse. The only word I can use to describe how I felt as a ten-year-old child being forced to watch such filth is icky. It made me feel icky. In viewing it, I cannot tell you that I understood much of what I saw, but there was a sick feeling in the pit of my stomach. I covered my eyes and looked away. I was instantly ashamed, even though it was not by my choosing. Something deep within me told me that it wasn't right. Now, some twenty years later, I am haunted by the things I saw back then. It is a constant source of prayer that I will keep my thoughts pure and if my mind travels back there, I immediately refocus.

Through the years, I became desensitized to seeing graphic images. I watched movies with illicit sex. I listened to music with sexually explicit lyrics. I had no qualms with seeing anything of a sexual or violent content. It all stemmed from having watched pornography as a child, as well as total disregard by my parents for what I viewed. It scarred me. I carried the shame around for years. Through counseling women, I have heard more stories of sexual abuse than I can remember or even care to. Each time a woman opens up and shares this horror, I am overwhelmed with compassion. My heart breaks for I know that it is a long journey through recovery. And it doesn't matter how much her family or friends think she should do it. Only she can choose to embark upon such a journey.

I was invited to speak at a ladies' meeting one Friday in the spring. I had finished speaking and the event was coming to a close. There was a woman in her mid-forties sitting in a chair across the room, crying softly. After the room cleared, I walked over to her and gently put my arm around her. She began to slowly share her story with me. I sat and cried with her as she released this heavy burden of sexual abuse. We held hands and prayed. Her story was so horrid that as I later drove from the parking lot, I had to pull over. I was physically ill at the thought of what so many women have to endure.

At another meeting, I was sitting in the back of the room as a young girl in her early twenties shared her story of having been raped as a teenager. As she brought her story to completion, she asked if anyone had any questions or comments they would like to share. A woman, perhaps in her fifties, raised her hand and began to share. None of us expected what we heard next. Tears streamed down her face as she spoke. She told the story of how she had dated the same man for over ten years and shared a child of with him. He had beaten her regularly. She was trying to leave him and had taken her daughter one night. As they began to walk a few blocks away to a relative's home, he followed her. He was furious that she was leaving him and he began to beat her in the street. She sent her daughter to run to the relative's home. The woman began to run, as her boyfriend hit her repeatedly in the face. He tackled her to the ground and she pulled a gun from her purse. He wrestled the gun from her and beat her across the face. He raped her in the middle of someone's driveway at only ten o'clock at night. As she told her story over the next fifteen minutes, you could have heard a pin drop.

After she finished, no one said a word. We sat in silence for several minutes. The guest speaker then asked if there were others in the room that had been raped or molested. Several nodded, and as we began to look around the room, more than seventy-five percent of that room had suffered such atrocities.

In this book, I chose to only mention a couple incidents of sexual abuse in my past. I did not go into details, give names, or recite every incident. I did this for a few reasons. One of the biggest reasons is that I have totally forgiven all the individuals that participated in those events. I harbor no anger or bitterness. I am living in total freedom over my past. The other reason is that the men I actually do mention are now deceased, the others are not. There were many more instances of sexual abuse that I could have talked about with more perpetrators. In fact, I could have written pages on the events. But I simply wanted you to know that I am a victim as well, and I got through it. That's the most important message you need to hear. I got through it and am healthy. You can, too.

For some of you who read my story, you could relate on many levels. Others of you have read in awe of why one person would take so much abuse. You wondered at some point, "When is enough, enough? When is she going to move on with her life and leave this guy alone? What is wrong with her?" Have you ever heard the saying, "You cannot see the forest for the trees"? I guess that is the best way to describe an abusive relationship.

Each time an incident would take place in my own relationship, I would vow that was it. I would be determined to end the relationship. And every time I did, he would come on stronger. It's like that, sometimes. As you try to end a relationship of any kind with a party that is not adding value to your life, they oftentimes will come back with a vengeance, wanting to convince you they are worthy of your time. For an abused woman, this can be the cycle that will not end. Because you have been through past abuse, your self-esteem is low. Your self-confidence is down. You cannot imagine yourself deserving better. Who would want you, anyway? Because you have those feelings, you begin to allow events to take place in your relationships that an otherwise healthy woman would not. You tolerate abuse. You settle for it.

As I look back through my past, one thing is for certain. I needed to be loved. Every time a new stepmom entered my life, I called her "momma" and embraced her with open arms. Later, I accepted every apology my boyfriend gave to me over his indiscretions. I needed someone to think I had value. I needed someone to love me. I needed to be validated, to feel I was worthy of such love.

According to an article published *by Aphrodite Women's Health* on March 14, 2007, fifty percent of all sexually abused children come from a single parent home. Thus, my passion for the betterment of single mothers overtakes me. How can I not address how to recover from this hurt? As single mothers who are victims of abuse, you can sometimes be so blinded by your own past abuse that you are not fervently looking to protect your own child. As sad as that sounds, we can fall into that trap very quickly. Many times, single moms are in such depression and loneliness that they invite a man into their home to fill that void in their lives, not thinking of the potential dire consequences. It only takes a minute for your son or daughter's life to be altered forever, so we must be fervent in our own recovery, so that we are healthy enough to properly raise our children and keep our wits.

In my own personal experience, as well as through the many women I have worked with, I have found a common thread. As abuse victims, it is easy to allow those events to shape the rest of your life. If you do not spend time healing, you will become obsessed with the event. You will think on it day and night. Your every decision will revolve around the abuse. You cannot effectively parent. You cannot function. It holds you hostage. Every relationship going forward is ruined or tainted. You manipulate your future relationships so that you will not have to deal with the hurt and pain inside.

Can I tell you that it will never end if you do not take control of it? When I think of my own journey through the healing process, I think of it as a step-by-step recovery. I did not magically transform into a healthy person. I did not even know that I was mentally unhealthy for many years. I was in my mid-twenties before I ever had the nerve to talk about it.

I strongly recommend counseling. In fact, I do not believe you can survive or truly thrive unless you do seek help. As a single mom, I know that money can be an issue in paying for such services. Begin to pursue your local church. Oftentimes, they have licensed or trained counselors on staff that can begin to work with you through your pain. If your personal church does not offer such support, then you can search for other area churches. You are not required to be a member at that church to receive help. Many local communities have free or nearly-free community counseling centers. Start somewhere. Do not put it off. Do not say that you do not have time. You do not have time *not* to get counseling. For every day that you put it off, you are losing precious time with your own children; time when you could be healthy.

You need to be able to release what you are carrying around. Once you talk about it, you will begin to slowly feel a burden lifted from your shoulders. You will breathe easier. This is not an overnight process. I do not want to give the impression that it is. I do not pretend to be an expert at the in's and out's of the human psyche. I can only speak to what I know is true in my own life and those that I have counseled. The more I have talked about my abuse, the more freedom I have experienced.

From the first time I uttered the words, I was free. The years of embarrassment began to slowly dissipate. For every time I shared my story, it could no longer suffocate me or hold me in bondage. I was no longer a slave to the thoughts that had held me captive. The weight of the world was off me. The same can be true for you.

The number one thing that I have lived with through the years is shame. Logically, I know that the abuse was not my fault. I could not have prevented it. I could have done nothing differently. But in the midst of my pain, I could not see that. I lived with the shame that somehow I was wrong. I was dirty. I wanted it. I lived with the feeling of being used goods, no longer wanted by anyone. What's worse is that I could not talk about it. I felt that no one would believe me. I thought I would be laughed at or made fun of. No one would care. I felt this was something that I should just "get over." So, I swept it under the rug for many years. Only now do I have the freedom that I once longed for. I carried this desire to share it, but lived in shame to say the words aloud. I no longer feel that shame and embarrassment.

In addition to counseling, you must have a strong prayer life. Prayer played an important role in my recovery. There were certain things that I knew no one else would understand or I couldn't bring myself to tell anyone else. I had to learn to lean on God. I spent many nights on my knees crying out to God with my pain. I asked repeatedly for help in forgiving those who had hurt me. I asked him to heal my pain, my embarrassment, and my shame. And little by little, he did.

I grabbed every book I could find on sexual healing from a Christian perspective. I was never much of a reader, but I found great healing through reading. I loved how I could read and then re-read a section or chapter until I got it. It was awesome to see how a particular chapter in a book would not mean anything to me at first, but as I grew in my recovery, it resonated loud and clear.

And lastly, you need a mentor, someone who has gone through abuse and is now recovered. This person will help keep you accountable to following your recovery plan issued by your counselor. She will also lend a shoulder to cry on during those crucial, but difficult facets of your recovery. We all need to lock arms with someone who is stronger than us that can help encourage us and lift us up. It's important that you know that your boyfriend (if you have one) cannot replace a mentor. He is not far enough removed from the situation. Be sure to pray about who God would have for you that can help you in your journey ahead.

There is no one thing that will allow your feelings or hurt to disappear. You must actively pursue your own recovery. Get the counseling you need. Pray. Read books. And get a mentor. Decide that it will take some time, but make the decision now. I know in the middle of your hurting that few words make a difference. I pray that as you read this chapter again and again that its words will begin to minister to your very soul, that somehow you can release some of the past pain. I know that as you find a counselor, mentor, and spiritual leader, such as a minister or pastor, to begin to confide in about these tragedies in your life, you will feel the same freedom I now have.

Scripture says in John 8:36, "Whom the Son sets free is free indeed." Amen. I invite you to stand on that word. God is telling you that there is freedom in Christ. He is saying that all the sins in the world and all the bondages that we often find ourselves in will not stand, if we truly get set free through Christ.

I do not pretend to know your exact story. I am not walking through your pain. But I am giving you hope that there is freedom from it all. I am encouraging you that you can get through it. I want to inspire you to search for that recovery, to reach for it. I want to give you hope that there is definitely a freedom in Christ. There is a place that you can get to where there is no more bitterness or un-forgive-ness in your soul.

Do not give up or give in. Rest assured. The road to recovery will get hard. But you cannot live your life in a bubble of defeat, heartache, and shame. Do it for your children. Do it for you.

OVERCOMING ABUSE
WEEK 1

Have you suffered with abuse, in any form, as a child or adult? Do you know someone who has? What are your thoughts and feelings about the abuse?

_____

_____

_____

_____

Oftentimes, women do not feel that verbal abuse is as harmful to them as physical or sexual abuse. Read James 3:6 and write it here. What does this tell us about our words?

_____

_____

_____

_____

Think about a time in your life when you were rejected. How did you handle it?

_____

_____

_____

_____

For many women, they carry abuse and rejection from their past for many years. Commit today to a plan of releasing this past hurt. Write your plan here.

_____

_____

_____

_____

_____

_____

_____

PRAYER:

Lord, I have suffered so much pain from the past that I cannot carry it anymore. I give it to you, today. Give me wisdom today as I begin to release hurt, pain, and bitterness. Direct my path on the next steps that you would have me to take for ultimate healing. Amen.

OVERCOMING ABUSE
WEEK 2

As we continue to discuss abuse, it is likely that you will deal with several emotions through this process. I recommend counseling. Write the names and phone numbers of local churches or community organizations that provide free counseling in your area.

_____

_____

_____

_____

It is crucial that we have friends to share our stories with. Was there a difficult time in your past that a friend helped you through? Describe it here.

_____

_____

_____

_____

Write the names of two or three close friends that you feel comfortable confiding in.

_____

_____

_____

_____

Is there anything that you are carrying from your past that you have not told anyone? How do you think you would feel if you shared it?

_____

_____

_____

_____

What is the number one thing you would like your children to know about abuse? What measures have you put in place to avoid abuse in your own home?

_____

_____

_____

_____

PRAYER:

Father, allow me to begin today anew. Allow me to make a new start. Give me fresh perspective. I ask for total freedom. I pray that I will continue to work on my own healing, so that I can be healthy for my children. Give me strength to endure my recovery. Amen.

CHAPTER 8

BEING A SINGLE PARENT

Change can be difficult. There is a transition that takes place when you become a parent, married or not. This change becomes far greater if you are moving into the single parent world and doing it all on your own. This book is written to encourage all single mothers: divorced, unwed, and widowed. The more I thought about each of these separate groups, the more I realized that no matter how you arrived at single parenthood this journey is going to be similar.

With the exception of widows, single parenting didn't happen instantly. It was a process. Whether you had an unexpected pregnancy or went through a treacherous divorce, we can all agree that it did not happen in the blink of an eye. If you had a drunken one-night stand or have had a long history of sex outside marriage (which likely stems from past hurt or abuses), it is safe to say that having a baby was not the plan. Or maybe you married Mr. Right and it turned out to be wrong. Regardless of whose fault the failed marriage was, we can again assume that you had not planned to parent alone. It usually takes many months and sometimes many years for a marriage to end in divorce. Consequently, becoming comfortable in the role of a single mom will take time.

Patience is the key. And if you are anything like me, this is a tough one. I am an instantaneous girl. I want whatever problem I am dealing with to be fixed and over before the sun goes down. That wouldn't require much patience, would it? You must give yourself time to go through the myriad of emotions you are undoubtedly experiencing. Allow yourself time to regroup and decide what path you are now on.

There are four common areas that I have found most single moms struggling with:

- financial burden
- emotional stress
- parenting concerns, and
- the pursuit of spiritual growth.

I dedicated an entire chapter to both parenting and finances, so I will address emotional stress and spiritual growth here.

I told you earlier about how I grew up in and out of church. I then discussed how I returned to church and developed a strong relationship with God. I cannot go further without telling you step by step how to become a Christian. For I believe whole-heartedly that I can give you all the parenting or financial advice known to man, but if you have not accepted Christ as your Savior, then you will still be unable to find true happiness.

Galatians 5:22–23 says, "But the Holy Spirit produces this kind of fruit in our lives: love, joy, peace, patience, kindness, goodness, faithfulness, gentleness, and self-control."

Love? "Love makes the world go 'round," they say. In the middle of parenting a child alone and trying to stretch a dollar to put food on the table, can you even fathom peace and joy? Most of you cannot. You want that peace, but it seems your whole world is flipped upside down. You may be trying to work three jobs to make ends meet. You may be rushing little Johnny from ball practice to band practice. You don't know which way to turn. You are tired. What about kindness and gentleness? Has there been a time when you were parenting that you wished you had been a little more kind and gentle with your toddler or teenager? Do you wonder what is wrong with you? "Am I the only parent on earth that screams profanities at my kids?" you may wonder. These are the things that God's Word says he will provide: peace, joy, and love.

Do you know that if I depended on my husband as my source, even now, I would be disappointed? I have talked about what an awesome husband I have. I have mentioned how he loves the Lord and puts him above all else. I talked of how he treats me like a queen. I also mentioned that none of us could be a perfect man or woman, but we can be the perfect one for our spouse. That's all true. No matter how hard my husband tries, there will be times when he makes mistakes, as will I. If I lean on him to be the source of my happiness and joy, then I lose. I come up empty. Does he bring joy into my life? Of course, he does. My children do. My friends and family also do. But none of those people are the source of my joy, peace, and happiness. Those things come from deep within my gut. Those things are rooted in my faith and only my heavenly Father can provide those things.

For some of you, you have gone through your whole life looking for the void in your heart to be filled. You have felt a hole. You have sought relationships that failed. You have been abandoned by family and friends. The church has failed you. You do not know where else to turn. The hole in your heart can only be filled with Jesus Christ. Let me be real with you. There is nothing wrong with you desiring to be married, be loved, and have the white picket fence with two beautiful children. God made us for relationships. However, when we look to another human being to be our source of joy and hope, we will always be disappointed. There is no man or woman on earth that can be perfect; no perfect friends, no perfect parents. We all strive to be those things, but only God is perfect.

In the midst of my drama, I always desired to be loved. Somehow, I thought having sex at thirteen years old would make me feel complete. It would make me feel loved. I thought partying all night at the local club scenes could mask my insecurities. I convinced myself it was fun. And maybe it was for a few brief moments. I moved from one relationship to another, finally settling into a seven-year relationship that I should have moved on from years earlier. None of it helped. I was constantly empty. I was not looking to Christ as my source.

You have to be whole in Christ. Your whole identity cannot be wrapped up in material things, such as clothes or shoes. And it cannot be wrapped up in multiple sexual partners or dancing all night at the clubs. I have seen women addicted to everything: shopping, pornography, sex, drugs, and alcohol. Some don't even realize the addiction. Usually from years of pain, they grasp at something to help ease their pain. When reaching for these things, they come up short. You must be complete, looking to God as your source of strength, in order to live a full life. Am I saying every day will be perfect with sunshine and roses? Will you never have trouble? I am not saying that. I am saying the Lord gives you hope that you can make it through. And the peace comes from deep within, not just some temporary high that we can get on from alcohol or drugs.

That's how God made us. He made us with a desire to be loved and to worship. Some of you (like me) have spent years worshiping men, sex, drugs, alcohol, pornography, or money. Yet, you always wind up feeling empty. You may not have referred to it as worshiping, and you may not have been addicted to it, but that thing, whatever it was, became your source of happiness. You have spent your life wandering from one self-fulfillment to another, and still couldn't understand why you weren't happy. You may have even tried the whole church thing. It is not church, not religion, but rather a relationship with Christ that delivers you true happiness.

I will share with you what I call Christianity 101—Bible basics. It doesn't matter what church you choose or what denomination you pursue. (Do your homework and pray that God will lead you to a good, Bible-based church where you can grow.) But the most important steps are as follows:

1. Recognize what sin is.

James 4:17 says, "It is sin to know what you ought to do and then not do it."

2. Recognize that you are a sinner and what the consequence of sin is.

Romans 3:23 says, "For everyone has sinned and fallen short of God's standard."

Romans 6:23 says, "For the wages of sin is death."

3. Repent. Believe Jesus is the son of God.

John 3:16 says, "For God so loved the world that he gave his one and only Son , so that everyone that believes in him will not perish but have eternal life."

John 14:6 says, "Jesus said, 'I am the Way, the Truth, and the Life. No one can come to the Father except through me'."

Romans 10:9–10 says, "If you confess with your mouth that Jesus is Lord and believe in your heart that God raised him from the dead, you will be saved. For it is by believing that you are made right with God, and it is by confessing with your mouth that you are saved."

It is as simple as that. You can become a Christian anywhere—in a church service or on your bedroom floor.

Once you become a Christian, you will want to learn more through God's Word, prayer, and church attendance.

I have seen women in their twenties that desperately search for something in their lives. They do not know exactly what, but something. Unfortunately, I see that same search for inner peace coming from women in their fifties and sixties. The search is not age specific. I see women jumping to the latest fad religion and losing interest in it after it does not bring the everlasting joy that they hoped it would. Here again, it's all about a relationship, not a religion.

As you are navigating through this season in your life, there is another big piece of the puzzle, emotions. I was thinking about the widowed mother and what devastation she must go through. I have experienced death, but never that of a spouse. When you look into the eyes of your children, I know you are at a loss as to the perfect words to say. But as I thought on that, I realized the same can be true of an unwed or divorced mother. It is not uncommon that grief would strike a mother who just lost a relationship that she thought was going to last. It is natural to mourn the loss of what could have been, what you hoped for.

Grief can move us right into loneliness and depression. Depending on the severity, depression allows our mind to play tricks on us. We start self-doubting. "I'll never find someone like Bobby," you may begin to think. "I'll always be alone. God doesn't have anyone for me. He doesn't care about me." You start thinking about all the things you could have done differently. You beat yourself up with coulda, shoulda, woulda's.

Bitterness, anger, and un-forgiveness are similar. They sneak up on you just the same way as loneliness and depression. You start by thinking about one incident that went wrong, one time that you were treated poorly, and it escalates to epic proportions. You think about every time your husband or boyfriend mistreated you, especially if you were abused. Everything angers you, past, and present. You are furious about your finances and aggravated about your children's disobedience. Be careful. You do not want to become a seventy-year-old, enraged, bitter, grandmother that people avoid like the plague.

> Get rid of all bitterness, rage, anger, harsh words, and slander, as well as all types of evil behavior. Instead, be kind to each other, tenderhearted, forgiving one another, just as God through Christ has forgiven you.
>
> Ephesians 4:31–32

Talk about wise counsel! Let go of all the bitterness, anger, and un-forgiveness. It will eat you alive, if you don't. Many times, we do not forgive because we want to hurt the other person emotionally. It always backfires. The sooner you can let go, the better.

Celebrate small accomplishments. If you had the urge to scream at your child and you didn't, then celebrate it (even if you screamed at him three hours later). Start with baby steps. Loneliness, grief, bitterness, anger, and un-forgiveness will take time to deal with, so be prepared. Reward yourself for all small victories. (If you are suffering from severe, on-going depression, seek medical help.) Finally, remember this is only a season of your life, a small window of time in your eighty- or ninety-year journey. Children grow up. They move away. You will make it through this time. Don't focus on trying to find a new man to have a new husband or dad for your children. God will handle that in his timing, if he desires that for your life. But do focus on being the best mother, friend, sister, and Christian you can be. When you do that, you will not lose who you are in this process.

BEING A SINGLE PARENT
WEEK 3

What are the four most common areas that single moms struggle with?

_____

_____

_____

_____

Which one do you feel is the most difficult for you? Why?

_____

_____

_____

_____

Read Galatians 5:22–23. Which of these qualities do you most desire in your life?

_____

_____

_____

_____

Write the most disappointing thing you have experienced during this transition to single parenting. Was it your fault? Whether you answered yes or no, release yourself right now from this disappointment.

_____

_____

_____

_____

Is there something that you have spent years addicted to, e.g. men, sex, drugs, money, alcohol, shopping, or partying? When you think about that activity, does it bring you true joy?

_____

_____

_____

_____

Write the three steps to becoming a Christian here.

_____

_____

PRAYER:

Dear God, I ask forgiveness for my sins. I have lived my life in a way that has not been pleasing to you. It has left me empty. Fill me with joy. I believe you sent your son to die for my sins. I want to change my life and live for you. Please help me. Amen.

CHAPTER 9

PLAYING THE VICTIM ROLE

I recently heard a pastor speak on truth. He talked about how the Bible is full of truth. The Bible says the truth sets us free. He went on to later say that there are times in our lives that it is easy to twist truth to fit our situation or make it comfortable for us, especially when we do not like what the truth really is. We have all heard that old adage that the truth hurts.

That statement will be true of what you are about to

read, so be prepared. You may ache a little after you read it. But it must be said.

First, let's talk about hurt. There are dozens of ways that you could have suffered hurt in your life. You could have suffered severe sexual trauma, such as rape or molestation. Maybe you have been beaten or verbally abused. Perhaps you grew up in a home with alcoholism or suffered through another traumatic event, such as death, divorce, or neglect. The list goes on and on. How we handle the hurt is key.

There is an appropriate time for dealing with hurt. The Bible talks about going through different seasons of life. It is healthy to mourn the loss of a loved one after a death. It is normal to have anger or hurt after you have been wronged or abused. That is appropriate and expected. Here is when we get into the danger zone, when we cannot move past the hurt. This is especially true for victims of violent crime or abuse.

I am not going to tell you what is an exact appropriate time to go through a particular emotion. What took me two months to recover from may take you two years. Each person grieves differently. Everyone has a process of recovery to go through. The aftereffects of divorce or abuse can be mind-blowing and take months or years to work through. The important thing is that you do work through it. The event will paralyze your life until you do.

For example, the loss of a child is devastating. I have known many people that have suffered such a loss. But I have also known women that ten years later are still mourning the loss almost daily. Is this to say that you ever stop missing the child or wonder what could have been of their life? Of course not. This was your child, your flesh and blood. They will always hold a special place in your heart.

The same is true for abuse. Let's say you were raised by a drug-addicted mother. She beat you and was sexually promiscuous. She verbally assaulted you on a regular basis. It is okay for you to have hurt and anger as you grow up. You are now an adult in your forties. What quality of life will you have if you do not deal with the hurt from your past?

I want to be extremely clear. I do not dare minimize the pain associated with death, divorce, abuse, and other trauma. Not at all. I have personally walked through most of that tragedy. It is tumultuous. It hurts. You are on an emotional roller coaster that does not seem to end. I have tremendous compassion for those suffering through those events.

But until you deal with the events, you are immobilized. You function through life fairly normal, but no one knows what you carry deep within you. When you do not seek out the necessary tools to help you, the event defines the rest of your life. It is not just a part of your life. It becomes your whole life. You become a victim, not a mom, sister, or daughter, but a victim only.

When we have had a rough childhood or hurt and abuse in our past, possibly from a previous relationship, it is very easy to slip into the victim role. We get so caught up in wanting to be right, wanting to seek revenge on those that hurt us, or wanting someone to feel sorry for what has been done to us that we do not give it to God. We lose focus. The past consumes us. We never move forward to the present.

Some of you cannot stop speaking negativity over your life. *I am too fat. I am not pretty enough. I do not have that great of a personality. I have no friends. My children never obey me. You do not understand how I feel. I was abused.* Stop doing that! When you do that, you begin to believe those things. They become your truth.

Consider the story of Job, as told in the book of the Bible by the same name. Job was considered a wealthy man in his day. He had a flourishing family and business. He was admired by his family and the community. He was considered a God-fearing man and was obedient to follow God's will for his life. He was righteous, a man of complete integrity. He was an all-around good guy. Satan approached the Lord one day about Job. He told the Lord that Job was only faithful because the Lord had prospered him greatly, but if the Lord took away all his wealth, then he would curse God. The Lord agreed to allow Satan to take away all of Job's wealth. He lost his business. Job continues to praise God, even though he has lost all wealth. Satan comes back again and is granted permission to take away Job's family, so they all died. He later takes away Job's health, and he becomes very sick. He still continues to praise God. Job's friends began to falsely accuse him of sin. They tell him that he must have done something to deserve this.

Job lost everything: family, friends, money, and health. Yet, he continued to praise God. He never blamed God. At the end of the story, God restores Job to far more than he had before. He raises up more children for Job. He gives him more wealth than he once had. His health is restored. Have you ever been in that kind of situation? Have you lost all your money? Your reputation? Your family? Use Job as an example in your own life. Job had two choices. He could blame God for his hardship or he could praise

God for his goodness. He could deal with his temporary hurt, knowing that God is always faithful to supply all our needs.

In my years of working with women, I have heard almost every story imaginable. I think of the woman who told me she watched her husband burn to death in a fire. I think of the seventy-year-old widow who endured thirty-seven years of physical beatings before her husband died. I think of the young girl who was raped and the rapist later approached her to deliver her undergarments back to her. I think of the breast cancer survivor who lost both breasts. Do you know what is amazing about each and every one of these women? They are all serving the Lord faithfully and have gone on to live happy, healthy lives after the tragedy. They have claimed their victory, and the chains of the event hold them no more.

Some of you just want to complain. You want someone to feel sorry for your situation, but you do not want to do anything about it. The bitterness and un-forgiveness are like a cancer that is eating you up, but you will not get che-motherapy. Do not think for one minute that I am ignoring what you have gone through. I understand. I know the hurt and pain of disappointment after disappointment. I know the pit we can sometimes find ourselves in. Sorrow comes in many packages. We hide it well. Well-dressed, rich, beautiful women have it too. The feat of parenting a child alone can be overwhelming, especially when most of us didn't plan it. We imagine the perfect home with a loving spouse, plenty of money, and obedient children. We imagine the perfect job. When those things don't happen, it is so easy to become absorbed in the pain.

There is a time for mourning. There is a time to grieve

for what you have lost, whether it is a death or a failed relationship. It is okay to miss that relationship. But you must realize that your personal joy is not someone else's responsibility. You choose to get up. If we are not careful, depression, loneliness, suicidal thoughts, feelings of inadequacy, self-pity, self-esteem issues, self-consciousness, and the feeling of being overwhelmed can sneak up on us. We look up one day, and we have nothing to live for. We cannot find joy. The joy of the Lord is your strength.

When it gets so bad that you literally do not know how you are going to pay the light bill, there is hope. When you aren't sure where your next meal is coming from, or how you can pay your house note, is sometimes our darkest hour. When we are overcome with pain over past hurt, we have to stand on the promises of God. We have to believe that there is hope. If we give up, then we are done. Our children have a fruitless life. Our children suffer. Don't you want to be the very best parent you can? Of course, you do. We all do. There is encouragement all over the scripture that we can cling to in the middle of our storm. Here are just a few:

> Daniel 6:26–27 ... For he is the living God, and he will endure forever. His kingdom will never be destroyed, and his rule will never end. He rescues and saves his people; he performs miraculous signs and wonders in the heavens and on earth.

> Isaiah 4:9–10 I took you from the ends of the earth, from its farthest corners I called you. I said, You are my servant. I chose you and have not rejected you. So do not fear, for I am with you; do not be dismayed, for I am your God. I will strengthen you and help you; do

not be dismayed for I am your God. I will strengthen you and help you; I will uphold you with my mighty right hand.

Psalm 57:2 I will cry out to God most High, to God who performs all things for me.

Matthew 15:32 Jesus called his disciples to him and said, "I have compassion for these people."

Through the above verses, we can find strength. God is telling us that he has compassion on us, that he loves us, and that he will not reject us. He wants us to lean on his strength. It is yours for the taking. All you have to do is ask him for it.

Proverbs 19:3 says, "People ruin their lives by their own foolishness and then are angry at the Lord." Ouch! I think we can all agree that as we have walked through this life there have been things that we have messed up and also things that were done to us. There were mistakes made. In the midst of these mistakes, we can be quick to blame God. We take our anger out on him. "How could you do this to me? Why me?" We may cry out.

Be careful not to live in blaming God or others for your situation. It does not matter if someone else caused it. When we blame others and carry the bitterness that it brings, we hurt. We do not cause harm to the other person. Along with blaming others, we sometimes blame God. I do not understand everything that happens on this earth. I cannot wrap my mind around why there are starving children or disease or why bad things happen to seemingly good people. I have been asked about those things many times by non-believers.

Here is my response. I turn to God's Word again.

> My thoughts are nothing like your thoughts and my ways are far beyond anything you could imagine. For just as the heavens are higher than the earth, so my ways are higher than your ways and my thoughts higher than your thoughts.
>
> Isaiah 55:8–9

God is saying He has all this under control. He tells us clearly that there are things we are not going to understand because he is far smarter and deeper than us. The depth of his knowledge is something we cannot even wrap our brains around! There is another scripture I have clung to through the years:

> All things work for the good of those who love the Lord and are called according to his purpose.
>
> Romans 8:28

For so long, I could not understand why I was molested. Why did my dad turn his back on me? Why was I the victim of an abusive relationship? Why? Why? Why? Well, I got tired of wondering why those things happened! It does not matter. It really doesn't. There is not one thing that can be done about your past. There is not one thing you can say that will change what has happened to you. The only thing that is different is how you handle your future. I made a decision to not let anything from my past control my future. I decided to not be bitter at God, but to accept that there were things that I didn't understand. Romans 8:28 is probably one of my favorite scriptures of all time. I quote it often. The Bible does not say that if you are a Christian that everything good will happen to you. It says that even the bad things will work out for your good in the end.

How has that happened for me? There is not one event in my life that has not shaped me to be stronger and more sensitive. The events have allowed me to reach out to other hurting women and help them. A long time ago I was faced with a decision of whether or not to continue to live in the misery that was my life. I chose to change it. I praise God for the strength that I needed to do that. I prayed daily for that strength and it did not happen instantly, but when it did, I seized it.

What is the alternative? Stop and think about it for a minute. If you do not seize God's word and begin the journey to recovery, what happens? You continue to question God. You continue to live in offense, looking for someone to hurt like you have been hurt. You look for someone to blame. The end result is complete misery. No one wants to be around you. You remain the victim. Praise God that he has promised us victory. Yours is there for the taking.

PLAYING THE VICTIM ROLE
WEEK 4

What has been the biggest source of hurt and pain from your past? How long ago did it happen?

_____

_____

_____

_____

Have you dealt with the pain? Why or why not?

_____

_____

_____

_____

Do you believe that this event has shaped your choices later in life? How so?

_____

_____

_____

_____

What do you remember about Job's hardships? What did he lose? How did he react?

_____

_____

_____

_____

Have you become obsessed with seeking revenge from your past hurt? Do you feel that it is important that everyone know about your past hurts and how they affected you?

_____

_____

_____

_____

Do you find yourself speaking about those events on a regular basis?

_____

_____

_____

_____

PRAYER:

Lord, please reveal to me areas of my past that I have not given to you. I do not want to live in the past. I do not want my past to consume me. Allow me to deal with this pain so that I can become the woman and mother that you want me to be. Amen.

PLAYING THE VICTIM ROLE
WEEK 5

Do you find that you are extremely hard on yourself? Do you say things like, "I am too fat. I am not pretty enough. My children never obey me. I am not a good mom."

_____

_____

_____

_____

Think of someone who has suffered tremendously in their life. Write their story here.

_____

_____

_____

_____

Is there someone who has less money than you? Poorer health? Begin to thank God for what you have. List some of your blessings here.

_____

_____

_____

_____

Have you ever wondered why you have suffered such hardships in your life? Write Isaiah 55:8–9 here.

_____

_____

_____

_____

Record Romans 8:28 here. Does this give you a new perspective on your past?

_____

_____

_____

_____

PRAYER:

Father, help me to be thankful for who I am and what I have. Help me to not focus on what I have suffered in my past. Keep me focused on my positive future. Amen.

CHAPTER 10
PARENTING 101

E very mom wants to be able to say, "I am very proud of my son/daughter." We want to watch our children graduate high school with honors, as the star athlete, and then move on to college. We want them to become doctors and marry the perfect person. We envision the best for our children, far more than we ever had. Even if you provide the best parenting you possibly can, there is no guarantee that your child will become all those things listed above. We do, however, want to do our best in helping Little Sally or Little Johnny achieve their best.

Proverbs 31:27–28 says, "She carefully watches everything in her household and suffers nothing to laziness. Her children stand and bless her."

Oh, to hear my children stand and bless me one day! What an honor as a mom. We all should aspire to such a blessing. Did you read what the first part of that verse says? She is not lazy. Good parenting takes effort. It is not easy. It is not free, but it is worth it.

How could I write a guide for the single mom and not discuss parenting? You could go to the local bookstore and purchase every parenting book available and still not have all the tools necessary to raise your child. Spank them. Don't spank them. Give them bedtime at eight o'clock p.m. Wait until ten o'clock p.m. Many books contradict each other. Perhaps you read through my advice and do not agree with all of it. But the following information is what I have found to be the most effective parenting skills for single mothers, based on my own experience, biblical teachings, and years of working with other single moms.

I have taught parenting classes to single moms for years now. Brace yourself for this one. I do not consider myself to be an expert. Most authors would never say such a thing. But this statement raises to mind the following question. Who is a parenting expert? How do you get that title? A PhD from Harvard? Perhaps. I, personally, would rather have coffee with a group of experienced mothers and discuss what they have found is working and what does not work with rearing children. I would rather listen to a grandmother who has successfully raised five productive children facilitate a round-table discussion on the subject. That is what this segment will be; what I believe works, based on my own experience, teaching and counseling, and God's Word. Envision me sitting with you having a discussion on your living room sofa. This is real talk for real women who need real help.

Ladies, it is time for a gut check. The fact that you are reading this book tells me you are looking for help and a way to grow as a single mother. Now is the time for self-reflection. You need to ask yourself some pretty tough questions that you may not like the answers to. Give yourself a few minutes to reflect on the following:

1. Do I have a relationship with Jesus? Do I understand what that means? Can I pinpoint a time in my life when I gave my life to the Lord?

2. Do I feel good enough? Do I feel worthy of love?

3. Am I happy where I am right now?

4. Do I believe that God put dreams inside of me? Am I taking steps to realize and live out those dreams?

The answer to all those questions must be an emphatic, "Yes!" If not, then you need to begin to work through each area that isn't. For example, since having a relationship with Christ is the key to having joy, peace, love, and patience, how can you effectively parent without a relationship with him? Don't you need those things to parent? What about being happy with who you are, and feeling good enough? If the answer is no, then you will have a hard time imparting positive emotions to your child. You have to work through those issues that prevent you from feeling good enough or that prevent you from dreaming of your future successes.

Let me explain it to you this way. As a single mom, you are super-busy. You could be attending school, working, or doing both. You may be working multiple jobs. In addition, you are caring for your child who has school projects, basketball practice, and a doctor's appointment. You are extremely busy with many things, and worrying about you is the last thing you should be doing, right? Wrong. The first step to effectively parenting your child is working on you. Just look at the emotional scars that many of us have suffered through based on our parents' mistakes in parenting, their inadequacies. If you are not a whole person (well-rounded, full of joy, and optimistic), then the task of parenting alone will almost be more than you can bear. Life does not stop when you become a mom, so continue to work on yourself.

Once you have begun to work on you, both emotionally and spiritually, then we can move on to some parenting do's and don'ts. When I began to think about starting a single mom's ministry, my initial reason for wanting to start it was to give parenting advice. Quite frankly, I had seen one too many ill-behaved children. While my own parenting was not flawless, I could see that my children were well-behaved and respectful. I wanted to give that to other women.

As I began the journey of working with women, I uncovered four common parenting mistakes:

1. Overindulgence out of guilt. This is a scary one. This is the most common of the four. Mom wants her child to be happy. She wants to do everything in her power to make that happen. Oftentimes, she feels guilty that somehow it may be her fault that Dad does not live with them or her fault that she chose Dad in the first place, so she caters to the child's every whim. Have you ever seen a child fall to the floor in the toy aisle of the local discount store, screaming and kicking because he wants the latest toy truck? Embarrassed, Mom leans over and quietly whispers, "Johnny, if you will calm down, then we will get the truck." Johnny gets up with a smile on his face as he walks away with the toy in his hand. Have you ever been that mom?

I have seen moms that are having serious financial difficulty purchase their children all the latest name-brand fashions, expensive electronic equipment (such as iPods , gaming devices, and cell phones), or throw them extravagant parties. This is done from guilt, guilt that she doesn't have the money to provide the same as Sally's parents, guilt that her child doesn't have a dad around, or guilt that the Jones family down the street is doing it.

Parents, in general, have this problem. I wouldn't be honest to tell you that I have never over-indulged one of my children. However, with single moms, it escalates ten-fold because there is no one else there to help balance out a poor parenting decision. You want your child to feel loved, and you become overcome with that desire, not realizing the negative implications. What is the result of such over-indulgence? Everyone knows about that spoiled-rotten kid from the neighborhood, or the smart-mouthed teenager that everyone avoids. That is the result. You will be raising that child. Constantly indulging your child's wants, whether money is an issue or not, leads to a lack of respect between you and your child. You become the ATM, not the parent.

Be strong. Do not give in. Your child will grow up ill-prepared for life if you always give in.

2. Failing to discipline. There are several reasons that a single mom fails to discipline her child. Exhaustion comes to mind. After carrying the weight of the world on your shoulders all day, it is much easier to just give in than to listen to them ask a dozen times or listen to a temper tantrum. Another reason for failing to discipline is fear of being the constant bad guy. Because you do not have the luxury of a second parent that can sometimes be the disciplinarian, you always must do it. You may want your child to love you, and it's hard to watch them be angry at you when you discipline. Lastly, many moms are unsure of how to discipline, so they simply do not do it. They are afraid of making mistakes or duplicating their own childhood, so they become immobile. Whatever the reason, you must discipline. Remember you are not your child's friend. You are his parent.

Your child craves structure and discipline from

a very young age. Anything less than that leads to rowdy, disrespectful children. You give your child the gift of love, security, and belonging when you discipline, and that is what true love is all about.

3. Being too strict leads to rebellion. Wow, have I struggled with this one! While you certainly do not want to be the pushover parent, there is a line that you do not want to cross into being too strict. Parental instruction should be given for protection and growth opportunities for your child. Be careful not to abuse your authority by becoming a bully. Because you cannot control that your rent is two months behind or that your ex-husband is not paying child support on time, it is easy to relay that frustration to your child. When you cannot control other things in your life, it is natural to want to control those things that you can. This method will backfire and usually leads to rebellious, confrontational children in the future.

Here is an example. My dad was a huge disciplinarian. He was too strict in many areas. He screened every phone call. Our bedtime was nine o'clock p.m. as high school students. He prohibited boys from calling our house (even as high school seniors)! We were never allowed to date. What did I do as a result? I began to sneak around behind his back and do it anyway. At seventeen years old, I was pregnant, yet I still could not date or have conversations on the phone with boys. Boys were the enemy in my dad's world. Rather than educating me about the proper behavior with them. He secluded me. His attempts backfired. Yours will, too.

4. Negatively impacting your child's character. Growing up, my dad would say to me, "Don't do as I do; do as I say do." Many parents still use that same approach today. After years of watching my dad in sexual immorality, is it any wonder that I began that same pattern? Moms, it is not good enough to merely tell your child not to engage in certain activities, you must be an example. It is important to first consider what type of character you want to develop in your child. When you think of a man or woman of high integrity, what words come to mind? Moral. Honest. Kind. Pure.

Your child is watching your every move. Ask yourself a simple question. "Would I want my child doing what I am doing right now?" This is an accurate gauge of how effective you are at being a good example for your child to follow. Do not think that your toddler or young child does not notice what you are doing. I have memories as early as two years old, as do most people.

There are dozens of areas where your child is watching you. I chose to name a few here:

- Sex. You are not fooling your child when you say, "Mr. Bob and Mom are going to have a slumber party, tonight." They instinctively know something is wrong. They may not be able to articulate it yet, but they know.

- Music, Internet, and television. Do you watch questionable television programs with foul language or illicit sex? Do you listen to music of the same description? What you feed your spirit becomes embedded in your thoughts. Would you want your child to repeat verbatim the movie you just watched? If not, cut it out of your life.

- Honesty. When you find $20 in the parking lot, turn it back into the grocery store manager. Do not reason that you really need the money. When you want cable television, do not run a wire from your neighbor's house. Buy your own or do without it. However minor these examples may seem, they provide excellent opportunities for you to increase your child's integrity. Do the right thing, even when it is difficult.

- Prejudices. Whether we are talking about racism, sexism, or economic status, we absolutely want our children to be free of such prejudices. Be careful not to categorize others based on the references listed above, but rather by the condition of their heart. If this is an area you struggle in, begin to pray that the Lord would give you a new way of thinking. Release any bitterness you have against another race or gender.

If someone says, I love God, but hates a Christian brother or sister, that person is a liar; for if we don't love people we can see, how can we love God, whom we cannot see? And He has given us this command:

Those who love God must also love their Christian brothers and sisters.

1 John 4:20–21

Now that we have cleared out the parenting mistakes, let us begin to discuss five ways to make you a better mom.

Step one is to recognize that you need help. You cannot do it alone. Yes, you are a single mom, but you must begin to lean on family and friends for occasional help. Do not be prideful. None of us can do it fully alone.

> Two people are better off than one, for they can help each other succeed. If one person falls, the other can reach out and help. But someone who falls alone is in real trouble. Likewise, two people lying together can keep warm. But how can one be warm alone? A person standing alone can be attacked and defeated, but two can stand back to back and conquer. Three are even better, for a triple-braided cord is not easily broken.
>
> Ecclesiastes 4:9–12

That is a pretty straightforward approach. Reach out to each other for help. Join a mom's playgroup. Join a Sunday school class. Start a Single Mom's Dinner Club to meet once a month. Form a babysitting co-op with other area moms.

Step two is allowing yourself some alone time. This is imperative. I know that it may not seem like a big issue, but it is. You must have time to regroup, when your world does not revolve around your children. There has to be quiet prayer time. For some, this may be a long bath after the kids are in bed. For others, you may awake before the children and get some quiet time in your room. Twice a month, take time to meet with a friend, counselor, or mentor. If babysitting is an issue, use the babysitting co-op mentioned in step one.

Step three is talking to your kids. From the time your infant is born, begin to talk to him. Sing to him. Praise him. As children grow, they need verbal affirmation from their parents. No subject is off-limits as they become older. Sex, financial matters, personal hygiene, and spiritual growth need desperately to be taught in the home first. All of these things are discussed at school and with friends. You do not want the drug dealer at a local convenient store to be the first one to discuss drugs with your child. Be bold. Open the door of communication very early and keep it open.

If you now have a teenager and you have not had an open line of communication, start now. It may be awkward at first, but keep working at it. Do not give up no matter what your teen's reaction. Start with an apology. "Sally, I am sorry that I have not talked with you as much as I should have through the years. I have let life get in the way. I have let my hurt over other things distract me. I love you. I want to begin our relationship again. Will you forgive me?" With persistence, this approach will pay off. It shows your teen that you are not above an apology and you care about them.

Avoid using foul language or screaming at your child. If you feel your anger beginning to rise to that point, walk away immediately. Your child's self-esteem is ripped down every time you scream. Be careful not to start this trend. Remember, they are watching.

Step four—dream. Do not allow life to beat you down to a point where you forget your dreams. We all have hopes, aspirations, and dreams. Sometimes, we are too scared to begin to talk about them again because we have suffered many disappointments in the past. We fear future rejection. You have a purpose. You may have dreamed of becoming a hairdresser or opening your own daycare center. You may desire to get a college degree so that you can teach school. Go for it. Stop listening to the negative thoughts and fears from the past. Jump into the new thing God has for you, the exciting thing.

Jeremiah 29:11 says, "For I know the plans I have for you, says the Lord. They are plans for good and not for disaster, to give you a future and a hope."

The best thing you can do for your children's dreams is achieve your own. You never want your son or daughter to look back and wonder why Mom never opened that restaurant she always dreamed about. Whatever your dream, it is achievable. There are many government agencies that assist in funding education for low-income families or provide childcare, so that you may pursue your dream. Non-profit organizations and churches all over the country have programs set up to help you start on your path.

Your children have dreams as well. Be an encourager. Foster an environment that allows your children to thrive. Build up your children by speaking positivity over them. Tell them they can do anything.

Step five is to change your community. Volunteer. In Pastor Dino Rizzo's new book, *Servolution* (Zondervan, 2009), he takes the call of serving to a whole new level. His church started out with only small opportunities. They gave away bananas or bottles of water to the public. They cut yards for single moms or widows. They served meals to the homeless. The more faithful Healing Place Church was to serve the community, the more God expanded their capacity to reach others. It is such a rewarding experience.

Maybe you are barely holding on to your apartment right now, as they are threatening eviction. Then go to the local homeless shelter and serve. Pray over their needs. If you have just been given a bad medical diagnosis, go to a local hospital or nursing home to visit with others. Although I have suffered tremendous abuse, it took me less than twenty-four hours of volunteering in a battered woman's shelter to realize that my abuse paled in comparison to the travesties some women have endured. Volunteering offers a new perspective. There is always someone that is worse off than you. There is always someone to serve. Volunteering takes your mind off your own problems and allows you to reach out to others.

Remember how we talked about developing your child's character? What better way than through giving back to the community could you teach him or her about integrity? When you think about wanting to have your son or daughter marry the perfect person for them, begin to develop them into the perfect mate for that future spouse.

Think about babysitting for a friend. Cook dinner for an elderly neighbor. Run errands for a widow. Bake cookies for the apartment building. Fold clothes for a neighbor. There are thousands of low-cost ways to serve.

As you can see, the name of the game is a balanced life. The more well rounded you are, the better chance you are giving your children for a successful life. Through all the mistakes we make, we learn and grow. Do not spend time worrying about your past. Do not dwell on your inadequacies. Don't worry that your child doesn't live in a large, two-story home with a white picket fence around the backyard.

The life you lead may not be the one you envisioned for yourself or your children. That is okay. Embrace where you are right now. Enjoy your children. Enjoy who God made you to be and trust that you have been given these children to raise because God knows you can do it and do it well.

PARENTING 101
WEEK 6

What is your primary goal as a mother? Do you effectively communicate that to your children through words and actions?

_____

_____

_____

_____

There are four common parenting mistakes that single mothers make. What are they?

_____

_____

_____

_____

Which parenting mistake do you most closely identify with?

_____

_____

_____

_____

How can you begin to work on that area of your parenting?

_____

_____

_____

_____

What is your number one fear as a parent?

_____

_____

_____

_____

Are there things in your life that you do that you would never want your child to do? How can you prevent your child from doing them?

_____

_____

_____

_____

PRAYER:

Lord, I want to be the best mom I can possibly be. Help me to use wisdom with my parenting. Help me to be sensitive to my child's needs without becoming too lenient. Help me to raise my child up to be all you have called him to be. Amen.

PARENTING 101
WEEK 7

As a single parent, you must have help. Read Ephesians 4:9–12. Who in your life can you lean on to help with parenting?

_____

_____

_____

_____

Alone time is crucial in parenting. Do not allow yourself to feel guilty about having that time. What in the last time you had complete alone time? What can you do to get regular alone time?

_____

_____

_____

_____

Do you talk to your children on a regular basis, other than giving them instructions? Why or why not?

_____

_____

_____

_____

Write down a dream you have for your future. What does Jeremiah 29:11 say about your future?

_____

_____

_____

_____

List ways that you can volunteer in your community with your children. How do you think volunteering will make you feel about yourself?

_____

_____

_____

_____

PRAYER:

Heavenly Father, help me to foster friendships with people that can help me to effectively parent my children. Do not allow me to be prideful. I will accept the help, when it is offered. Help me to begin to dream again about my future and the future of my children. Thank you that you are changing me from the inside out.

CHAPTER 11
SURVIVING FINANCIAL CRISIS

I awoke one morning and began my morning routine. I showered and dressed. I brushed my teeth, and then reached for my contact lenses. I opened the container and accidentally ripped the lens in half with my fingernail. Since this was years before disposable lenses were popular, I did not have a replacement pair. I reached for my old glasses that were fitted with an expired prescription. Although they were the size of my grandmother's glasses, which covered half my face and I could barely see with them, they would have to do.

I cried all the way to work that morning. As I sat at my desk crying, my boss came in and asked, "What's wrong?"

I began to cry uncontrollably. Through tears, I muttered, "I ripped my contact lens this morning and I do not have the money to replace it, so I had to wear this ugly pair of glasses. Tomorrow is my daughter's second birthday, and I do not have the money for that either. And to top it all off, my car is acting up."

He paused for a moment and then asked, "Is there anything else going on?"

Puzzled, I said, "No. Isn't that enough?" I knew that he did not understand. I did not mean that I was struggling a little and that funds were low. I meant that there was no money, none. There was not some rainy day fund hiding away in the mattress somewhere. I had no emergency money for when the car broke down or the refrigerator was acting up. There was not a 401k account that I could borrow from temporarily. I mean, I had to count pennies to put $1.08 gas in my car to get to work. My boss was a wealthy business owner who came from a family of influence. He was a kind and compassionate boss, but I knew he did not understand the depths of my poverty or what it did to me emotionally.

With all my other troubles, it seemed financial burden was just one more thing added to my shoulders. I was doing everything I could to keep my head above water financially, but it seemed to never be good enough. I was tired of being so frugal with my money and still not having enough. I was exhausted with doing it all on my own. Would it ever get any better?

Many of you have probably heard 2 Timothy 6:10 which says, "For the love of money is the root of all kinds of evil." It sure seemed evil when the landlord came for my rent every month! Obviously, we need money to function, but we want to be careful that we do not cross the line of loving it, and all it stands for. In some ways, I equate money to food. We need it to survive. It is important, but when we start loving it, there are consequences to follow.

There was a time in my life when I was obsessed with money. It was all I could think about. I was going to college to earn more money. I worked extra hours to have extra money. *If I only had more money, life would not be so difficult,* I thought. And there is some truth to that. Of course, life is easier when you do not have to spend time wondering where your next meal is coming from, or how you will pay your car note. I agree. What I did not realize at that time, though, was even if someone threw millions of dollars at me, it still would not have been enough to make me happy.

Isn't it ironic that when some of the most successful Hollywood actors are interviewed by magazines or television reporters, their responses are often similar? They seldom speak of their overwhelming happiness. In fact, many of them speak about loneliness, depression, drug addiction, and failed marriages. Yet, many of us spend our lives in pursuit of an extravagant lifestyle with an overflow of financial wealth similar to that of a movie star.

The Bible does not say that money is evil. It is a necessity for us to function in society and be productive at what we have been called to do. It is the love of money that is evil. Jesus says in Matthew 6:24, "No one can serve two masters. For you will hate one and love the other; you will be devoted to one and despise the other. You cannot serve both God and money." He is not saying you cannot serve God if you have money, but rather it cannot be the master of your life, your focus, or source of happiness.

Having said all that, you still have bills to pay, groceries to purchase, and children to send to school. All of which cost money. The next several pages are designed to help you work through your financial difficulties with simple tips and direction. Because single moms vary in age, experience, and financial circumstances, I want to start with the very basics of money.

Part of my financial woes early in life was ignorance. We had only a modest income growing up. No one had taught me about how to open a checking account, much less balance one. I did not know much about budgeting or credit bureaus. These things were all equivalent to a foreign language. Most high schools do not offer classes that specifically cover money basics. If you do not learn it at home and it is not offered in school, where do you learn about finances? I know that is where some of you are. If you were never taught, then you are flying blind. You simply do not know. This chapter is designed to help you know.

TITHING

When I transitioned from my late teens to early twenties, I had hit rock bottom. I was working a job with no potential for promotion, raising two children on food stamps and welfare, with no end in sight. I had supported my children, at one point, on approximately $400 per month. The next job I took doubled my income, and I was making approximately $900 per month, which was wonderful to me, but still not enough to get off government assistance.

This is when the principle of tithing was re-introduced into my life through a sermon at church. As I said earlier, I had grown up attending church, and I am sure I had heard about tithing. However, I did not remember much. After hearing this particular sermon on tithing, I wrestled for some time with the concept. *How am I supposed to give the church my money when I can barely pay my bills?* I would think. Though I had my reservations, I could not get it off my mind, so I just did it.

Tithing may be new to you, so let me introduce it, here.

Then, Abram gave Melchizedek a tenth of all the goods he had recovered (Genesis 14:20).

One tenth of the produce of the land, whether grain from the fields or fruit from the trees, belongs to the Lord and must be set apart to him as holy. (Leviticus 27:30).

You must set aside of your crops—one-tenth of all crops you harvest each year. (Deuteronomy 14:22).

Bring all the tithes into the storehouse so there will be enough food in my temple. "If you do,' says the Lord of Heaven's Armies, 'I will open the windows of heaven for you. I will pour out a blessing so great you won't have enough room to take it in! Try it! Put me to the test' (Malachi 3:10).

From the beginning of scripture, we are instructed to give ten percent of our increase to God. That means, if you receive $500 weekly, you give $50 to God through your local church. Here is where it can get real tricky for us. Some of the thoughts I had (and you may be having) were, "I cannot afford to do this. That sure seems like a great deal of my money. I bet the pastor wants a pay raise or a new car!"

> And don't give reluctantly or in response to pressure. For God loves a person who gives cheerfully. And God will generously provide all you need. Then, you will always have everything you need and plenty left over to share with others.
>
> 2 Corinthians 9:7–8

First, the Lord calls us to be cheerful in our giving. He calls us to give only ten percent, while leaving us in control of the other ninety. It is all his anyway. This is not because God needs our money. All heaven and earth belong to him. This is a test of our faith and obedience. As for the pastor needing a pay raise or a new car, God commanded the tithe. Your pastor did not come up with the idea. Some pastors even avoid speaking on the subject for fear the congregation may think such thoughts. If it is true and funds are being misused, let God deal with that. This does not relieve you of your obligation to tithe.

Lastly, do not think you cannot afford to tithe. You cannot afford not to! As seen in the scriptures listed, the Lord is telling us to try him. He will provide all our needs and pour out blessings on us.

As I released the fears about tithing, I became faithful in my giving. I never looked back. I began to experience financial freedom in its fullest. Within months of tithing,

I landed a new job, for which I was not qualified, in my opinion. I began earning more than one thousand times my prior annual income. How does that happen? It was not that I no longer had bills. I simply no longer worried about them. I knew God was going to provide. I did not worry about how or when, because I stood on that truth of knowing he would, in his perfect timing. I got off food stamps and moved from government housing. I was finally able to purchase a car that did not leave me stranded on the roadside regularly.

It is important for me to stop and note that God is not our magical genie. We do not rub on the lamp and begin making demands. The same is true for tithing, attending church, or reading your Bible. Those are all great things that we should do, but they are not tools used to barter with God. He will provide what we need and sometimes what we want in His timing, when it is best for us, not when we demand it, through a desperate prayer.

I spent several years making more money than I could have ever hoped for or imagined. I vacationed in exotic locations. I took a cruise. I ate in fine dining establishments. I purchased a large home and a nice automobile. Those were all things that I believe the Lord blessed me with through my obedience to tithe. However, that is not where the story ended. There came a time in my life several years later when the Lord tested my obedience, once again. He called me to leave my position as a successful executive and volunteer full time with single moms. I would love to tell you that I dropped everything and immediately obeyed. I did not.

After over a year of contemplating how we would make it financially, I finally obeyed. The Lord gently reminded me that he was my provider and while my company had been a blessing to me, it was not my source. It was now time to move on to a new season of my life, leaving behind the things of old—money and all. I jumped into ministry with both feet, working with single mothers, having coffee with them, doing lunch, and praying with them. I began doing speaking engagements, all for free. Not once has a bill been unpaid in my home. This new season has given me the opportunity to be more resourceful in my spending, more conscious of what I spend, and to learn more about discounts and coupons. All of those things have allowed my ministry to flourish more. Those were things that single moms needed to know, so God allowed me to learn first.

BUDGETING

Now that you understand tithing, let's talk about budgets. Budgeting is another necessity in money management for the single mom. Many of us were not reared in lavish surroundings, so it should come as no surprise that adding children into a single-parent household will require some belt-tightening.

It is imperative, whether you are recently divorced or newly expecting, that you have your own checking account. The first step in budgeting is to know exactly what income enters the home and what leaves it. The easiest way to track this is via a check register. Be sure you inquire about a free checking account, as most banks now offer them. When you begin receiving monthly checking account statements, be sure to balance them (review your statement to match it against your check register ensuring totals match).

After opening a checking account, the second step to budgeting is to list on paper every bill you owe. This includes: housing, utilities, car notes, insurance, food, gas, school expenses, and any others that remain unnamed. Some expenses may need to be estimated, such as gas or food, until you begin to know what you spend every month. List debtors by payment, balance, and interest rate. A sample list is below:

MONTHLY OBLIGATION		BALANCE	INTEREST RATE
Mortgage note	$800	$100,000	9%
Car	$400	$12,000	12%
Credit Card	$25	$500	21%
Department store	$10	$300	28%
Daycare	$400		
Utilities	$400		
Gas	$300		
TOTAL	$2,335/ month		

For the next thirty days, list every penny you spend on paper. If you buy a cup of coffee, list it. Nothing goes under the radar. Be diligent. At the end of the thirty days, sit down and assess your financial situation. Did anything surprise you? Are you spending more on gas than you anticipated? Have you bought more magazines or coffee than you bargained for?

Some important items to note when tracking your income are as follows. Number one: be sure to count food stamps, welfare checks, or government rental assistance as income, if applicable. However, do not count bonuses, commissions, or sporadic child support. These are less predictable forms of income and should never be counted on, but rather viewed as a blessing once received.

I have counseled hundreds of people through financial crisis. The one thing that always surprises me is even though someone recognizes that they are having financial difficulty, they still do not have a budget on paper and oftentimes do not know what they owe. This is a must. You cannot begin to improve your finances if you do not know exactly where you are with them.

Let's start by comparing your list of monthly obligations to what you actually spent in the last thirty days. Are there some things not listed on your monthly obligations? Of course, there are. We all make purchases that we are not obligated to make, but rather, we choose to make. For example, we are obligated to pay the rent or we will have nowhere to live. However, we are not obligated to go to the movies with our best girlfriend on Friday night. This is when priorities begin to change.

Do not stop with the thirty-day evaluation. Keep a notebook or running total of all income and expenses. You will begin to accurately assess how much you need for groceries, gas, and diapers. This allows you to more closely budget what you can afford to spend on each. Speaking of what you can afford, now is time to introduce a new word: over-spending!

No one wants to hear this word, but we all need to. Let me explain to you the difference between needs and wants. Needs are food, housing, transportation, clothing, diapers, and toiletries. You need to pay for insurance or gas. Those are all needs. Wants are manicures, haircuts, eyebrow waxes, movie nights, restaurant expenses, and new clothes, shoes that are on clearance, and anything else that you do not absolutely have to have to survive. Clothing is listed under needs and wants. How can that be? Let me clarify. You need to have clothing to go to work in. You do not need to visit the mall because they are having a sale on all the latest fashions. That is a want. Let me take it a step further.

Transportation is a necessity. You must be able to get your children to school and you need a way to work. Whether you are using public transportation or have your own car, you must budget for such an expense. However, you do not need a new BMW. You may want one. They may look great, but you cannot justify it. Manicures? "Oh, but you do not know what my nails look like if I do not have a professional take care of them," you may say. Haircuts? Do you get your hair cut at the top salon in town or at the local Budget Cuts down the street? Yes, I know Bob at the salon has done your hair for years, but you may no longer be able to afford him. Do not misunderstand. We all enjoy getting special treatments and purchasing new clothes. However, when your budget is extremely tight, you cannot justify the purchase of that new outfit, no matter what percentage it was marked down on the clearance rack.

This may seem like such a simple concept for many of

you. I hope it is. But for many others, it is a huge struggle. I have had countless single moms approach the ministry and ask for assistance with their finances, but when I further evaluate their situation, they have chosen to not scale back their way of living. We find a lifestyle that we are comfortable with, but when life changes, we change with it. Your budget may no longer afford you the opportunity for that daily cup of coffee at the local bistro. The purchase of diapers may be your new obligation. This is when we must tell our children "no" to the huge birthday extravaganza or the new outfit. Perhaps, they cannot join in a particular activity at this time. That is okay. You are teaching them responsibility. Accept it now and you will have a much smoother transition.

As you begin to eliminate some unnecessary expenditure from your life, you will find that budgeting is much easier. Maybe you spent $4 per day on coffee. This would equate to $120 per month or perhaps you saved $30 by purchasing your shoes at the thrift store versus the mall. Every dollar saved can be reallocated, no matter how small it may seem.

Where do we apply these newfound funds? Refer to your budget again. Do you remember how I asked you to list interest rates of all debt owed, including balances? Begin to apply whatever extra you have found in your budget to that debt. You will never have financial freedom when you are drowning in debtors. This leads to our next topic.

CREDIT BUREAU REPORT

I still find it ironic that in my early twenties, I was counseling people about their finances, when I was living on food stamps and welfare. God certainly has a sense of humor, doesn't he? Credit Bureau Reports were one of those things that I learned about early in my financial counseling career. I can remember wondering why no one had shared this information with me before and how people functioned financially when they did not fully understand how their credit report worked. The sad thing is that many people ruin their credit report in their late teens and early twenties, before they even understand how it works.

Credit Reports are used in several areas of life. Most people know that they are used to assess your credit worthiness by a lender for future lending for items such as homes and automobiles, as well as personal loans. However, were you aware that your credit bureau can also be pulled in conjunction with an application for employment? Did you know that many landlords will not rent to a tenant without a copy of the tenant's credit bureau? Automobile and homeowner's insurance companies often require a credit report to be pulled.

As you can see, your credit report follows you for the rest of your life and in many areas that you perhaps never thought about.

Psalm 37:20 offers interesting insight into what the Bible says about debt. "The wicked borrow and never repay, but the godly are generous givers." The Bible is very clear about what our responsibilities are to our lenders.

"But what if my current credit situation is not my

fault?" you may ask. That is an unfortunate situation that many of you may find yourselves in. Maybe you allowed your ex-husband to pay all the bills and handle financial matters for your home. Perhaps an ex-boyfriend abused your kindness and used your credit cards to acquire debt you were not aware of, or left you holding the bag with payments. Maybe you co-signed for a friend who never paid the debt.

First of all, let us use the above-mentioned scenarios as learning experiences. At no time should either spouse have sole control over the finances. This prevents an unexpected death from leaving one spouse clueless. It also allows both spouses to pray about financial matters together. Single moms are much more susceptible to the other scenarios, particularly as it relates to boyfriends. In general, single moms desire to have someone to care for them for a change. They have given so much of themselves to caring for their children that at the end of the day they want to be hugged and feel that they are being taken care of.

It is when this guard is down that we can sometimes be manipulated into co-signing for a boyfriend who does not have acceptable credit or even lending credit cards for a charge that he promises he will pay. Both examples are recipes for disaster. Ask yourself the obvious questions. "Why doesn't he have acceptable credit, if he always pays his lender on time? If he is going to pay me back, why can't he just save for the item and purchase it at a later time?" Moms, guard yourselves. Do not allow your emotions to entangle you in a financial catastrophe. Ultimately, you are responsible for any purchases made in your name.

There are three things that I have often seen as the

cause for unsatisfactory credit ratings. First, individuals over-estimate their ability to repay based on what they perceive their financial status is versus what it really is. For example, you run out and buy the new dress at the local department store because it is on sale and Little Johnny's kindergarten graduation is coming up. You charge it on a credit card and say, in passing, "I get paid next Friday. I'll just pay it off then." Inevitably, five other things come up, and before you know it, there are dozens of small purchases made that are sitting on credit cards that you simply cannot pay. Do you remember me discussing over-spending? This may be a good time to review that section.

Secondly, individuals are hit with unexpected medical expenses. If you are reading this and have never had a medical emergency, be aware that it can financially ruin you! Please purchase medical insurance. It is not a luxury. It is a necessity. Most employers now offer health insurance. Do not decline that option. Another option is government assistance, which some of you may qualify for. If neither of those options is available, pursue a local insurance agent and find out what your options are.

The last most common reason for unsatisfactory credit ratings is divorce. Many of you find yourselves there today. You were unaware of the family's financial situation. You entrusted your ex-husband to take care of those things and he did not. Or, maybe you both overspent, over-estimated your ability to pay, and did not save for a rainy day. Whatever the reasons for your credit situation, we must now deal with it.

Obtain a copy of your credit report. You are entitled to a free one every year. They are easily ordered on-line. Once received, begin to contact creditors that you have not paid.

If you charged a credit card when you were eighteen and never paid it, you still owe the debt. No matter if you are now twenty-eight. Make it right. Begin to diligently work with each creditor to repay your debts. The same is true for medical bills. If you can only afford $10 per month, then make that offer to the lender. If you must use income tax returns to pay the debt, do it. Do not make plans for new purchases with extra money you receive, until you have diligently paid every lender what is due. This is what is right. Remember. You are teaching your children integrity. I caution you in not becoming bitter about paying a debtor that was an ex-spouse or ex-boyfriend's responsibility. If the debt is on your credit, pay it. Do not waste any more time hoping that he will do what is right. It will not help your credit situation. And you can use it as an opportunity to teach your children character.

It takes a great deal of time to begin to repair a poor credit report. Be aware of agencies that claim to repair your credit in thirty days for $499. You must pay the debts. Your credit scores will not change overnight. But the daunting task of detangling your credit problems will not go away, so begin today.

COUPONS AND DISCOUNTS

This is an area that has been a true adventure for me through the years. As you will remember, I went from making a substantial amount of income to $0 annually. I was working full-time on a volunteer basis. With my husband now as the sole provider of our family's income,

I decided to become creative with our income and thus, I was introduced to coupons.

In Matthew 25:14–30, Jesus shares the parable of the loaned money. Three servants were given money by their master and made choices about how to handle the money. One servant invested his money and doubled it. Another servant went to work and doubled his money as well. However, the last servant buried his money in the ground, fearing he would lose the money. The story ends with this dramatic conclusion in Matthew 25:29. "To those who use well what they are given, even more will be given, and they will have an abundance. But from those who do nothing, even what little they have will be taken away."

We are all called to be good stewards of what we are blessed with. Finances may be extremely difficult for you right now. But, hold on. You be faithful. You continue to be diligent with your tithing, paying your debtors, and stretching your budget to its fullest. There will be a new season for you. I do not know when, but I know that Malachi 3:10 promises you favor. When I entered the world of coupons and discounts, I knew that was exactly what God was teaching me; to be a good steward with what I had. Because of what I have learned, I now know that I will not go back to spending more than necessary for groceries or toiletries. That is money that I can use to bless a single mom, or sow into our church ministries, or serve a homeless meal.

I have heard countless single mothers tell me that they simply did not have the time to clip coupons or that they did not know where to begin. Let me first tell you that with the new organizational information available on the web, you do not have to clip them until you need them. Watching your favorite television program while clipping coupons doesn't seem so bad if I tell you that you could save as much as 90% on your grocery budget, is it?

Many moms are unaware of all the discounts available. First, let me tell you that coupons can and should become your best friend. Do not pay full price. There are coupons for restaurants, movie theaters, and groceries. Begin to purchase your Sunday paper. Begin to print coupons from the Internet. Follow blogs that highlight savings in your local area. Free samples are available from every major discount store in America and can be accessed at their websites. I once used free shampoo samples for over thirty days when funds were limited on the family's toiletry budget for the month!

Major drug store and grocery retailers, such as Walgreens, CVS, Rite-Aid, Winn-Dixie, Albertsons, offer discounts, bonuses, and reward points to frequent shoppers. Many of these stores even offer rebate programs that allow for free items every month.

Begin to think about the amount of money you spend on food, soap, diapers, cleaning products, and toilet paper. It adds up to significant amounts of money. If you can get many of those items for free or at discounts of up to 90%, would you consider spending some designated time every month to researching the savings?

Stephanie Nelson is The Coupon Mom and hosts the website www.thecouponmom.com. Since 2004, she has appeared on Good Morning America, The Oprah Winfrey Show, The Today Show, and countless others. She shares her secrets and tips on how to save on everything. Her website will provide you with detailed information on how to get started. She offers a free e Book called *Cut Your Grocery Bill in Half with the Coupon Mom System* at www.coolsavings.com. Her website provides a chat forum where you can ask questions and chat with other frugal moms. She provides free information on coupons, restaurant savings, discounts, rebates, free samples, and holiday and back to school savings.

When I began using coupons and discounts, as well as rebate programs, I saved hundreds of dollars for my family. I saved $400 monthly just by using coupons and strategically watching for sales at local grocery stores. I began to carpool with friends when necessary. I began to plan my weekly trips to the market and post office so that they coincided with other errands to save on gas. I used store brand products when feasible. I realized that I did not have to be brand-faithful, and it saved me money. I became diligent about turning lights off around the house or not having our air conditioning system cooling too low in our home. Every area of our finances where I could cut back, I did. Eventually, I saved our family over $1,000 monthly by making only simple changes. You can, too. Search the Web. There are thousands of websites and blogs now available to help with money savings. Search for books and magazines with money-saving tips. There are dozens of television shows that offer great tips for the frugal parent. In addition, many churches are now offering coupon classes to help their parishioners save and budget. So, get started.

EMOTIONS

Discussing money evokes many emotions. I understand. Some of you continue to deal with feelings of inadequacy or failure. You feel that you have failed in a marriage, failed as a mother, and failed at finances. Now, you are entrusted to raise a child alone. You feel ill equipped for such a mighty task. You have not had much experience with handling finances and fear failure in that area as well. When using words like inadequacy, fear, and failure, depression can quickly approach. I encourage you with this word. 2 Timothy 1:7 says, "For God has not given us a spirit of fear and timidity, but of power, love, and self-discipline."

You do not have to fear your finances. Do not let past failures determine your future action. This verse tells us that he has equipped you with power—yes, power. He has equipped you with love, and then, there is self-discipline. You have already shown great discipline to get this book and begin to change your life. The challenge will now be for you to become self-disciplined with your spending and budgeting habits. There is no doubt that you can.

As you finish this chapter, I hope that you begin to feel elation. I want you to be excited about what you are learning as a single mom. I want you to embark on each new area of your life with hope and expectancy. Look at what you have learned so far. Use the skills that you are learning now to change your life. Be a new mom with excellent money-management skills, who can stretch a dollar further than she ever thought could. Begin to teach your children about money as they grow, so they do not repeat any financial mistakes you have made.

For further information on how to become free of financial struggles, I refer moms to Dave Ramsey. Dave Ramsey is a financial expert who has authored numerous books. He hosts his own radio program, The Dave Ramsey Show, which reaches millions of listeners weekly, and he is a well-known television personality. He offers financial advice from a Christian perspective. He has been featured on The Oprah Winfrey Show, CBS, 60 Minutes, and The Early Show. He is the creator of Financial Peace University, a thirteen-week video series offered to adults and teens across the country to teach about financial matters, such as savings, credit, and giving. His series has been featured in hundreds of schools and churches.

Refer to his website www.DaveRamsey.com for dozens of resources, including a full list of his books and times for his radio program, to assist you in your new walk towards financial freedom.

SURVIVING FINANCIAL CRISIS
WEEK 8

Write down what you understand about the principle of tithing. Is this a new concept for you?

_____

_____

_____

_____

What does 2 Corinthians 9:7–8 say about giving?

_____

_____

_____

Take time right now to list every bill you owe. Include all debts and monthly utilities. You must keep track of every penny entering and leaving your home.

_____

_____

_____

_____

_____

_____

_____

_____

_____

In reviewing your budget, what areas can you cut back in? Have you been guilty of over-spending? Commit today to live on a very tight budget during this transitional time. Pray for God to help you.

_____

_____

_____

_____

Look at your budget again. What is the smallest debt you owe? Begin to work towards paying it off. What plan do you have to do that?

_____

_____

_____

_____

PRAYER:

Lord, I commit my finances to you. I will be faithful to tithe ten percent of my income to you. I am committed to changing my spending habits and being a good steward of all you have given me. Amen.

SURVIVING FINANCIAL CRISIS
WEEK 9

What are three areas in which a Credit Bureau Report is used in your life?

_____

_____

_____

_____

Write Psalm 37:20 here. What does this teach you about your debts?

_____

_____

_____

_____

What are three potential reasons for unsatisfactory credit ratings?

_____

_____

_____

_____

Order a copy of your credit report online through Transunion, Experian, and Equifax. In the meantime, begin making a list of any creditors that you know you owe and their phone numbers. Begin to contact them this week about paying those debts.

_____

_____

_____

_____

_____

_____

_____

_____

Explore the world of coupons and discounts. Over the next thirty days, list one magazine, newspaper, or internet source per week that you find useful in helping to save your family money.

_____

_____

_____

_____

When you think of your current financial situation, list the emotions that come to mind.

_____

_____

_____

_____

PRAYER:

God, I am determined to positively impact my financial situation. Help me to remain faithful in paying off all the debts I owe. Keep me motivated to take action with my finances. I pray that I will not become overwhelmed or discouraged. Amen.

CHAPTER 12

HERE WE GO 'ROUND THE MULBERRY BUSH—CYCLES

Stop and think about your life for a moment. Think about how you grew up. Are there things that happened to you as a child that still affect you today? Have you repeated some of the mistakes that your parents made? Have you repeated the same mistake more than once?

We all have had a friend (or been the one) that drinks too much, parties too hard, or moves from one meaningless relationship to another. She may use drugs or watch pornography. She always seems to be the life of the party. She may even experience periods of time when she is genuinely happy with her life. Then, she crashes. She hates life, hates men, and hates herself. And she swears to never drink, smoke, do drugs, or party ever again.

It usually isn't long before she is back at it again. Do you ever wonder why she cannot stop? Are you the girl that cannot stop, and you are frustrated and wonder why?

Any time you have a great night at the bar or dance club, drinking and partying, it always ends. Always. When you wake up the next morning (usually with a great deal of regret about what you did the night before), all you have to show for it is a hangover and some momentary happiness. Many people spend their lives on this emotional roller coaster. Everything is great. It is wonderful. Then, in the next moment, life is terrible. Bobby hates me. I need a drink.

The fact that you are a single mom already opens you up to many unfavorable statistics. Single moms are more likely to have children who become single parents. According to a University of Chicago study sited by CNN in November, 1999, seventy-eight percent of the prison population were raised by single parents. That same study states that the children of inmates are twenty times more likely to go to prison themselves. Cycles.

Alcoholics produce alcoholics. My dad was an alcoholic who loved to hang out in the bars all night. My mother was killed by an alcoholic. Ironically, I found myself, only a few short years later, drinking too much and driving home drunk. My father was verbally abusive to me as I grew up. When I had my own children, I began that same pattern of using profanity and screaming at my children. More cycles.

I have counseled women that are on government assistance, who represent four generations of families on government assistance. I have worked with many young girls who gave birth at thirteen or fourteen years old, only to find out that their mothers and grandmothers were also teen moms. I have personally witnessed dozens of cases of generational abuse. The grandmother beat the mother. Now, the mother beats her daughter, and so on. Cycles! Cycles! Cycles!

We never plan to get caught in the middle of bondage, bad lifestyle choices, and vicious cycles of abuse. A woman never plans to become a prostitute. It wasn't her lifetime dream. A drug addict did not believe that her first puff of marijuana would lead to addiction. As a mom, you never plan to abuse your children. A young girl who grew up watching her mother get beaten over and over again by her boyfriend vows to never be the victim of such a crime. Yet, all of these things happen frequently.

And, they happen slowly, often without us noticing.

Verbal, emotional, physical, and sexual abuse is commonly repeated through generations. Alcoholism, grief, depression, single parenting, poverty, and sexual promiscuity can also lend itself to generational cycles. Cycles destroy our future. They destroy our hope for tomorrow. They limit us from seeing where we can go because we only see where we came from, what Momma was, what Daddy was.

Sexual sin is one of the strongest bondages affecting us today. The subject is often avoided. Many churches avoid talking about it for fear that they will alienate their congregations. Parents do not talk to their children about it. Yet, it is the raging beast that so closely binds many of the other cycles; alcoholism, single parenting, financial destruction, depression, etc.

1 Corinthians 6:18–20 says, "Run from sexual sin! No other sin as clearly affects the body as this one does. For sexual immorality is a sin against your own body. Don't you realize that your body is a temple of the Holy Spirit, who lives in you and was given to you by God? You do not belong to yourself for God bought you with a high price. So you must honor God with your body."

Here are some statistics directly related to sexual immorality:

- 22% of all pregnancies end in abortion (Stomacher Institute, July 2008).

- From 1978–2008, more than 45 million babies have been aborted (Guttmacher Institute, July 2008).

- Almost 37,000 people per year are diagnosed with AIDS (reported by State Health Departments, 2008).

- More than 70% of men between eighteen to thirty-four years old have viewed pornography (SafeFamilies.org).

- Sixty-seven percent of divorce is directly related to infidelity (MenStuff.org).

- The average age a woman gets into prostitution is age fourteen. She stays in it an average of eleven years. Eighty-two percent of all prostitutes were raped (U.S. Department of Justice, 2007).

Movies and television glamorize sexual immorality to make it appealing to the viewer.

Anything goes. Do what feels right. Read the statistics above again. Does this feel right? The facts above are staggering, but they do not address the even bigger problems. They do not talk about the depression, loneliness, insecurity, and trauma that the individuals are left with after poor choices. In spite of the emotional damage, in spite of God's word, and in spite of the statistics that vehemently support avoiding sex outside of marriage, we still continue to pursue this bondage.

So, how do we stop this? How do we stop running to the very things that have made us, our parents, and many before them miserable? You must first recognize what is going on. Recognize that you are in the midst of a cycle. That is the hardest part. Many times we see our parents get abused or be the abuser. We see them become alcoholics, so we secretly think that is going to be us in twenty years. Even statistics support it. Why is that? It is very simple. We condition ourselves to expect less. We begin to see ourselves just like our parents were. Although we are told over and over as children that we can do anything or be anything, we simply do not believe it. In fact, I would venture to say that some of our parents did not believe it. In my years of counseling, I have seen the mother of a young child say, "Brian that is wonderful. Of course, you can be an astronaut! You can do anything!" But once life has taken a toll and she has had hardships of her own, I have seen that same mother say to her son, now slightly older, "Brian, sit down and shut up. You are not going to be anything but a factory worker just like your loser father was!"

As mothers, we must be extremely cautious of what we

speak over our children. Your child's future depends on it. Your child can be anything. She can do anything. And guess what? You can, too. Stop believing that you will always live on government assistance. Do not accept less than God's best for your life. Begin to see yourself as a daughter of the King of Kings. Demand better for yourself.

I was driving across town the other day and began to turn the dial of the radio to different talk shows. I finally landed on a financial advice talk show, although I am not sure who it was. He made a comment that I found interesting. Studies have shown that most people are only as wealthy as the average of their five closest friends. Isn't that amazing? Since you have decided (consciously or subconsciously) that you will never make more money than your parents did or that your friends do, then you won't.

You have already seen three generations in your family become alcoholics, so I guess that means you are going to fall into that pit also. Your grandmother and your mother were single moms. You are a single mom. Doesn't that mean that your daughter is doomed to more of the same? No.

Consider Emily. I worked with Emily for over a year. She came to me two months pregnant. She had been a drug addict for over ten years. She was raised in a violent home by a mother who was addicted to drugs. Her mother began to give her drugs at a young age. Although I have seen drug addicts and abuse victims many times, there was something about Emily that just drew me to her. She seemed like an innocent young girl who just needed to be loved.

We began to invest time and resources into her. She went through a drug rehabilitation program. She began to go to church two or three times a week. We monitored her visitors closely. We threw her a surprise baby shower. She developed close friends through the church. After the birth of her baby, she enrolled in college and began to look for a job. She seemed to be going on the right track.

Within weeks, she had reconnected with her old boyfriend. She began to smoke and drink the first night she was with him. The drugs quickly followed. Before I knew what was happening, I lost complete contact with Emily and later learned that she was back in drug rehabilitation only a few months later.

Nikki was a twenty-year-old college student who came to me at six months pregnant. She had completed thirteen drug rehabilitation programs. She, too, seemed to be a sweet, innocent girl who had been caught up with the wrong crowd. She had moved from several states away, so I felt good about her future. She had separated from the wrong influences in her life. She went through the pregnancy drug-free. She began to attend church and had plans to complete college and work in the medical field. Nikki gave birth to a healthy baby girl. Within forty-eight hours, she was released from the hospital and went home with her newborn. She asked her father if she could borrow his car to make a run to the grocery store for diapers. She disappeared. We later learned that she had connected with a new boyfriend and was high on drugs again. Her mother eventually took that baby to raise.

Emily and Nikki broke my heart. With each woman that comes through my door, I believe the best for her. I truly believe that she can change her life. I believe that her past is now behind her and begin to look toward her future. So, why did they both go back to drugs? The problem was that they did not believe their lives could be different. They were both raised in drug-infested homes with lackluster parents. No matter what they said to me, inside, they believed that they would go back to their old lifestyles eventually. As much as I loved those two girls, I cannot believe hard enough for them. They have to believe they can change. They must see themselves as new in Christ.

Cassie was different. Cassie came from a similar background as Nikki and Emily. She used drugs, became an unwed mother, and lived in her car. She came to me tired and scared with few friends, on the verge of financial ruin. She, too, dedicated her life to the Lord and became committed to attending church and Bible studies. There was something in her eyes that made me know that she was serious. She began slowly to speak up during Bible groups. She volunteered with the local church. She began to ask new friends out for coffee. Now, more than a year later, she is financially flourishing, drug free, sexually pure, and employed with an outreach that serves other single mothers. Her story is one of the many successful stories that keep me motivated to continue the journey.

What makes her story different from the two others? Cassie truly believed she could do it. She believed that Christ's power in her life was sufficient to cover all past hurt and mistakes.

The great news is that the Bible says that is available for anyone. We do not have to be bound by our parents' choices. In fact, we do not have to be bound by our own poor choices from the past.

Second Corinthians 5:17 says, "This means that anyone who belongs to Christ has become a new person. The old life is gone; a new life has begun!" This means you have the freedom to make new decisions. You no longer live in the bondage of who you were before you became a Christian. That's exciting news, right? You decide what the outcome of your life will be on how you choose to live. Choose life.

CYCLES
WEEK 10

Is there a situation from your childhood that you have since repeated in your adult life, such as alcoholism, abuse, screaming at your children, financial irresponsibility, or sexual promiscuity?

_____

_____

_____

_____

Sexual sin can devastate us both emotionally and physically. List a few ways here.

_____

_____

_____

_____

What does 1 Corinthians 6:18–20 say about sexual sin?

_____

_____

_____

_____

Has there been a time in your life when you have spoken negativity over your children? Have you said things that you did not mean? Have you been a poor example to them? Take the time to ask forgiveness from your Heavenly Father and your children now.

_____

_____

_____

_____

Read 2 Corinthians 5:17. Do you believe that you are a new person in Christ?

_____

_____

_____

_____

PRAYER:

Lord, help me break the cycles that have held me captive in my family. I refuse to repeat another poor choice. I ask for your guidance with my choices.

CHAPTER 13

WHOM THE SON SETS FREE ...

As we come to the end of our journey together, I pray you have learned a great deal about yourself. We have covered everything from finances to parenting with many roads bridged in between. It is only fitting that I end the book with freedom. As you embark on this new life of parenting alone (and have just learned some new skills to do it), it is important that you feel empowered to move on. You need the confidence to persevere. Freedom offers you such confidence.

Freedom in Christ is the tie that binds every area we have talked about. We must be free to parent effectively, free to manage our finances appropriately, and free to relinquish emotional fears and doubts.

This country affords us such things as Freedom of Speech and Freedom of Religion. Thank God for those things. Thank God that we can go to church on Sundays. We can open our Bibles as we wish. We are free to worship in the streets, if we choose. All those things represent freedom. But what is true freedom?

There is one of two places where you live your life: freedom or bondage. There is not a halfway point. You do not straddle the fence with one leg in freedom and the other in bondage. Many words or phrases come to mind as I think about freedom and its opposite, bondage. This should give you a clearer picture of one's emotional state with each list.

BONDAGE	FREEDOM
Suffocation	Joy
Shackled	Peace
Confusion	Happiness
Fear	Fearless
Anxiety	Uninhibited
Hindered	Running & Skipping
Ashamed	Sun on my face
Embarrassed	Wrapped in a warm blanket
Addicted	Forgiveness
Slavery	Guilt-Free
Bitterness	Wings
Chains	Wind blowing through my hair

As you read through each list, is there one that you most closely identify with? Which list would you prefer to identify with?

In order for you to adequately understand freedom, it is crucial for you to understand bondage. Through the years, I have discussed Christianity with many people. I have had comments, such as, "That Christian thing is just too restrictive. I cannot live my life that way," or "I will live my life for Jesus in a few years, when I am older and settle down. Just let me find a husband, first." I remember thinking many of the same things in my teen years. For years, I thought that God just did not want us to have any fun. I have since come to a deeper understanding of what God wants for us.

Think of it in this way. As a mother, you love your children more than words can express. You have watched them grow from infants, to toddlers, and into adolescence. As they grow, there are times we must say no. For example, Johnny wants to climb onto a cabinet to reach the cookie jar. Sarah wants to go driving with her friend Susie, who has already been in two wrecks this year. Jonathan wants to go to a party where there will be no adult supervision. Your child's immediate response very well could be, "Mom never wants me to have any fun. She just wants to control me and make my life miserable."

God is our heavenly Father who created us. He loves us. He desires for us to live lives full of happiness, joy, and fun. In order to do that, there are things that he must also disapprove of. Rather than looking at things as restrictions, I challenge you to look at them as hot burners on a stove that you do not want to touch. If ignored, they can hurt you and leave permanent scars.

Why are we to stay away from drugs and alcohol? They lead to a path of destruction in our bodies. Have you ever seen someone addicted to drugs, whether on television or in person? We have been given one body to care for to the best of our abilities. Feeding our body poison would not be the best way to take care of it. God already knows that for whatever temporary enjoyment drugs and alcohol could offer, there is a lifetime of pain associated with it.

Pornography offers the same type of bondage. As you watch one smutty movie or glimpse at one inappropriate picture, you may wonder, "What's the harm?" Pornography has destroyed many marriages. It distorts our view of what should be meant as wholesome and pure. Once we have viewed such things, it is almost impossible to remove the images from our mind. One glimpse usually leads to two or three, then daily, then hours on end. It is an addiction of the worst kind, as most people are too ashamed or embarrassed to admit to the addiction. There is such shame attached to it. As with most addictions, the addict only admits there is a problem after their whole world is destroyed—loss of spouse, job, family, and money.

Sexual immorality is another big one that I hear arguments supporting. "Well, I love my boyfriend and it is not like I am with anyone else. I am faithful to him." "I have needs." "I am lonely. I do not want to be alone. He will not stay with me unless I do." "I just want to have some fun. I have earned that right. I have been a good girl all my life." There are hundreds, if not thousands, of statistics that support reasons to avoid sexual immorality, STDs, AIDS, and unplanned pregnancies. How fun is it when that man that you have physically given yourself to decides that he is no longer interested or he becomes unfaithful? Any loneliness you felt prior to a sexual encounter will not be cured with it. In fact, the likelihood of having a more severe bout of loneliness after he leaves you is almost inevitable.

Lastly, think about lying and deceit. When you begin entangling yourself and others in a web of lies, there is no end in sight. We all know the drill. You tell a little white lie to avoid an uncomfortable situation. Then, you must lie again to cover up that lie. Before you know what has happened, you are immersed in a sea of lies of which you cannot remember the truth. It leads to an internal war. It leads to an uncomfortable feeling in the pit of your stomach.

Every area above leads to emotional torment and bondage. Our Father in heaven does not want that for us. He wants us to enjoy our lives. The emotional consequences of choosing to live a life outside of God's will leave us in a state of confusion, unrest, and unhappiness.

Consider the following verses:

I will walk in freedom, for I have devoted myself to your commandments (Psalm 119:45).

For you have been called to live in freedom, my brothers and sisters. But don't use your freedom to satisfy your sinful nature. Instead, use your freedom to serve one another in love (Galatians 5:13).

And you will know the truth, and the truth will set you free.

But we are descendants of Abraham, they said. We have never been slaves to anyone.

What do you mean, 'You will be set free?' Jesus replied, I tell you the truth, everyone who sins is a slave of sin. A slave is not a permanent member of the family, but a son is a part of the family forever. So if the Son sets you free, you are truly free (John 8:32–36).

I want to jump out of my seat when I hear this! It cannot be plainer . The Bible explains to us that there is no freedom in living a life of sin. We wind up deeper and deeper in misery. Because God designed us, he knows the intricacies of our spirit, our emotions, and our physical wellbeing. We must trust that he has our best interest at heart, just as you love your children and have their best interests in mind. Freedom comes from knowing you are fine not to accept that invitation to become involved with drugs, alcohol, pornography, sexual immorality, or deceit.

When I think of living a life in total freedom, I think of peace. Peace in the world means there is no active conflict, no war going on around you. There can be complete peace all around you, yet a war rages internally. You are haunted by a past hurt or offense. You are living with a past sin that you cannot forgive yourself of. You want to choose the right thing, but you keep doing the wrong things, it seems. God's peace is confidence in any circumstance.

The secret to God's peace is to appreciate His perfect timing. Let's see what the Bible says about timing:

For everything there is a season, a time for every activity under the sun. A time to be born and a time to die. A time to plant and a time to harvest. A time to kill and a time to heal. A time to tear down and a time to build up. A time to cry and a time to laugh. A time to grieve and a time to dance. A time to scatter stones and a time to gather stones. A time to embrace and a time to throw away. A time to tear and a time to mend. A

time to be quiet and a time to speak. A time to love and
a time to hate. A time for war and a time for peace.

Ecclesiastes 3:1–8

Some of you need permission right now to move into a
new season. I am telling you that for some of you, that new
season is here. There is a time to cry and a time to mourn,
but you will notice that those are followed by times of
laughing, dancing, and mending. Understand that being
at peace with God's timing does not mean that you love
every minute of it. It does not mean that you enjoy the
learning process you are in. It simply means that you are
at peace to accept that God is in control, that He will take
care of it, and you will be just fine.

When you go through deep waters, I will be with you.
When you go through rivers of difficulty, you will not
drown. When you walk through the fire of oppression,
you will not be burned up; the flames will not consume
you.

Isaiah 43:2

That is a comforting word . Some of you find peace in
knowing God is with you to help you through your trials, but for others of you, you cannot accept this peace.
You cannot accept God's love. You are bound up with the
thought of, "But you do not know what I have done in
my past." This is when you discover that we all have different areas that we must gain freedom. You need to walk
through forgiveness. What are some different areas of forgiveness available to you?

FREEDOM TO GIVE AND RECEIVE FORGIVENESS

As Christians, we talk about how God forgives us of our sin. We talk about how much God loves us and how wonderful his grace and mercy are. But if you do not understand the depth of His love and mercy, you can still struggle with the concept of not being good enough. For some, your past has tormented you. It is eating you alive, gnawing at you day and night. Some of you are disgusted by things you have done, things you have seen, or heard. I have good news for you.

> Can anything ever separate us from Christ's love? Does it mean he no longer loves us if we have trouble or calamity, or are persecuted, or hungry, or destitute, or in danger or threatened with death? No, despite all these things, overwhelming victory is ours through Christ, who loved us.
>
> Romans 8:35, 37

Your guilt has overwhelmed you. You have lived in embarrassment and shame. But God is saying to you today, his victory overwhelms us. Do not dwell on what you have done wrong. Ask forgiveness from your heavenly Father and to those whom you have offended (whether they accept it or not) and move on. Accept his forgiveness.

The flip side of receiving forgiveness is giving forgiveness. Giving forgiveness is for your benefit. You are not granting forgiveness for the benefit of the other person.

The inability to forgive in itself is bitterness. You are grant-ing forgiveness so that you can move past the offense. I have seen many, many people allow un-forgiveness to age them beyond their years. Bitterness causes not only the physical appearance to change, but the emotional wellbe-ing to shrivel.

Let me release you of a potential fear you may have. Forgiveness does not mean acceptance of the offense and it does not mean trust. You are not saying that what you have endured is okay. You may have been raped or molested. Maybe you were beaten or abused. Perhaps you had a spouse that was unfaithful or suffered with an addic-tion, such as alcohol or pornography. You may be raising your child alone because his father abandoned you. None of those things are acceptable behaviors. Your forgiveness merely means that this event no longer dictates the rest of your life. You are a whole person in Christ and can hon-estly forgive the offender.

Do not wait on someone to ask for forgiveness. For-give others before you are asked. Truthfully, you may never receive such a request. Your offender could die, be impris-oned, disappear, or simply have a hardened heart. You do not want to die in bitterness and un-forgiveness. What kind of life does that offer you? What will you have gained by harboring un-forgiveness for the rest of your life? Will you have in some way hurt the one who hurt you? No, but what you will have done is lived a life in bondage to that un-forgiveness. We are talking about living a life of freedom.

I challenge you with Luke 23:34. "Jesus said, 'Father, forgive them for they do not know what they are doing.'" Right before Jesus was killed, he asked his father in heaven to forgive those who were putting him to death, the soldiers who spat on him, the Jewish leaders, the Roman politicians, and bystanders. Jesus is our ultimate example of forgiveness. As he hung on a cross, drowning in his own blood, dying a slow death, guilty of nothing, he forgave those who had hurt him. He did not wait for them to ask for his forgiveness.

FREEDOM TO ACCEPT DISCIPLINE

Accepting discipline can be a bitter pill to swallow if our hearts are not right. Just as it is necessary for you to discipline your children appropriately, it is also necessary for our heavenly Father to give such discipline. This gives us further evidence of his love for us.

Proverbs 3:11–12 says, "My child, don't reject the Lord's discipline, and don't be upset when he corrects you. For the Lord corrects those he loves, just as a father corrects a child in who he delights." When we ignore discipline, we back ourselves into a corner that is hard to get out of.

I can look back in my own life and see these truths so evidently. As I mentioned earlier, I have attended church most of my life. I have been taught biblical principles from early childhood. I understood that children are to obey their parents and that sex before marriages is wrong. Yet, I chose to move in the wrong direction in both those areas. When I was caught as an early teenager disobeying my dad's instructions and pursuing an unhealthy relationship, I did not ask for forgiveness. I secretly plotted on how I would be more aloof the next time. My thought was, *How can I not get caught again?* Not *What can I learn from this mistake?*

My first sexual encounter did not lead to pregnancy, but it was my inability to accept discipline and learn from my mistakes that ultimately did. Because I was unwilling to accept appropriate teaching and discipline by both my earthly and heavenly fathers, I have since walked out the consequences of mistakes made twenty years ago.

Oftentimes, we are overflowing with pride and arrogance, and simply do not want to admit to a mistake. We fail to accept discipline, because we will not admit there was ever a wrong-doing. We gloss over it. We pretend it never happened.

Proverbs 19:3 says, "People ruin their lives by their own foolishness and then are angry at the Lord."

Imagine how your life would be if you were free to accept discipline from your heavenly Father, your earthly parents, your boss, or even a mentor. When we have a receptive spirit and are open to receiving correction, we grow. Parenting our own children has much more to do with our heart towards God and our ability to receive correction, for how can we give correction and not receive it?

FREEDOM OVER ADDICTION

1 Corinthians 10:13 says, The temptations in your life are no different from what others experience. And God is faithful. He will not allow the temptation to be more than you can stand. When you are tempted, he will show you a way out so you can endure.

Praise God! He is saying that he will never give us something we cannot handle with his help. We have already discussed the destructive lifestyle that addiction can bring about. There are times when the pressures of the world may come down on you so heavy that it feels like you cannot take it another second, but take heart. God's word is true and he is promising you that when you are tempted, there will be a way out.

One thing that I have seen surface repeatedly when dealing with addiction is manipulation. The addict manipulates others into believing he wants to get better. He manipulates situations and circumstances so that he can feed his addiction in private. In fact, I have found that as time passes, addicts do not even realize they are manipulating friends and family. He can even manipulate the church into believing that he wants a new life. Be aware of this. Ask forgiveness from God and others if you have used manipulation to feed your addiction.

As an addict, you may not recognize if you are being manipulative. Begin to ask yourself some key questions. "Do I really believe what I just said, or do I simply want to be right?" "Do I have the desire to always be in control of every situation?" "Is this an issue that needs discussing, or am I turning this into an argument to avoid the real issue?" "Am I willing and ready to change my current lifestyle, or am I saying I want to change to buy more time?"

Once you have made up your mind that you are tired of the lifestyle, the destruction that your addiction causes, then you begin the process of achieving freedom over it. Seek help immediately. Do not wait a few days or few weeks to see how you do on your own. The longer you wait, the easier it is to fall back into the addiction trap.

Call your local church. Counselors are usually available and equipped with useful recovery information for addicts that range from substance abuse to pornography and beyond. Many cities have free group therapy and even have licensed therapists available at discount rates.

Let's not pretend that it is an easy journey, for we all know it is not. But the end result is a lifetime of happiness and freedom that no pill or drink could ever give.

FREEDOM TO NOT BE RIGHT

If I had to choose one area that has been an on-going struggle with me (not that there have not been many), this would be it. I have strong convictions and opinions and desire to have everyone agree. I believe there may be one or two of you out there that suffer in this area as well, so I offer you my thoughts.

I have spoken to you throughout the book about the job I landed after I began tithing back in my early twenties. I spent almost ten years with the company. I know that the Lord orchestrated me being there, and it was by his grace that I obtained such an immeasurable blessing. I will be forever grateful for all the things I learned there. My success with the company allowed my confidence to soar. My presentation and public speaking skills skyrocketed. My income increased dramatically. All of those were direct results of training from that company.

However, with increased confidence came increased arrogance and a total lack of humility. This was a gradual process. I won an award or received a promotion. I was called upon to speak to my colleagues during a presentation. Before I knew it, I had become extremely arrogant. I knew that I was good at my job and could not take direction well. If I was approached by a superior about changing a procedure, I became defensive. I argued with colleagues, supervisors, and other departments. I was always right. When it came to my management style, it was similar. I ruled with an iron fist. Employees dare not question my directives, or they would be sorry! My intention was never to become difficult. It happened because it was more important for me to be right than to maintain relationships.

I had a conversation with my beloved aunt one day. My aunt has been a Christian all her life and has been married to the same man for over fifty years. She has been a mentor, prayer warrior, and close friend for many years. I do not remember what started the conversation or what else we spoke about, but I did retain one key sentence. She said, "In the many years that I have been a Christian and maintained a marriage, I have learned one thing. It is more important to maintain the relationship than it is to be right. You give up your right to be right when you forge relationships."

She never knew how deeply that affected me. I was married to a caring, loving man, who was God's gift to me, and I never conceded an argument. I was always right in marriage, parenting, and business. Even now, I can remember how off-putting that was for others. I have since learned that the words of wisdom my aunt offered that day were far more valuable than any gift she could have given me. I treasure them even now.

There is nothing wrong with having strong convictions. There are injustices that should anger us. Our reaction to these convictions and anger is where the freedom comes in. I have now learned that every wrong in the world does not have to be righted by me. I do not need a cause to fight for, just for the sake of fighting for a cause. Every conversation does not need to end in an argument or a submission that I am the queen of knowledge on every subject. And I am okay with that. Whew! What freedom!

FREEDOM TO TRUST IN THE LORD

Do you remember falling in the love for the very first time? Maybe it was a high school sweetheart or a college classmate. Do you remember how you wanted to spend every waking moment getting to know him? You wanted to know about their family, their beliefs, as much as you possibly could. Let me challenge you with a different question. What about your heavenly Father? Do you want to spend time with him getting to know who he is and what he's like?

Many claim to believe in God or even love him. Yet, they never step foot inside a church, read their Bible, seek his will for their lives, or pray. Would that same approach to a new relationship work in your dating life? God knew you before you were even born. He knew you would make mistakes and he chose to send his son anyway. We all come from different religious backgrounds. Even among Christians, there are differences of opinion and different denominations. However, as I have said many times before, being a Christian is not about religion or some rituals that you perform every Sunday. It is about a relationship. God gives us freedom from religion in order to experience true relationship.

Relationships take time to develop. You must get to know one another. You do not end a relationship with a boyfriend, husband, or even a family member because something does not go your way. Then why is it that so many give their lives over to God (half-heartedly), and when He does not answer their prayers immediately in the way they see fit, they decide that this God-thing is not for them?

> When Pharaoh finally let the people go; God did not lead them along the main road that runs through Philistine territory, even though that was the shortest distance to the Promised Land. God said, 'If the people are faced with a battle, they might change their minds and return to Egypt.' So God led them in a roundabout way through the wilderness toward the Red Sea. Thus the Israelites left Egypt like an army ready for battle.
>
> Exodus 13:17–18

To give you a brief background, the Israelites were slaves to the Egyptians and had been severely mistreated through many years of bondage. God chose Moses to deliver the Israelites to freedom. Pharaoh would not let the Israelites leave willingly, so God sent a series of plagues to Egypt that tormented the Egyptians. Pharaoh finally relented. This is where the scripture above picks up. After having been beaten and abused for many years, one would think that the last thing on the Israelites mind would be to turn around and go back. However, as we see above, God knew that they would want to go back if they encountered trouble. Isn't that true of us all? When the going gets tough, we sometimes want to tuck our tails and run rather than see what wonderful thing is in store for us on the other side. Sometimes, even if there is something better ahead, we want to run back to what we know, what is comfortable. The key to freedom is pressing past this point.

Trusting in the Lord does not mean we have it all figured out. In fact, quite the opposite is true. The freedom comes in accepting that you will never have it all figured out, even if you spent the rest of your life in church every Sunday and attended Bible college the other days of the week.

> My thoughts are nothing like your thoughts," says the Lord. "And my ways are far beyond anything you could imagine. For just as the heavens are higher than the earth, so my ways are higher than your ways and my thoughts higher than your thoughts.
>
> Isaiah 55:8–9

This is one of the best ways to explain it. God has it all figured out and our job is to obey, not question, him.

There have been times in my life when I was wrapped up in a number of the bondages we have discussed. The problem was that I did not realize it. I could not figure out why I did not seem to have the true joy that Christians talk about, that the Bible talks about. The joy comes in making the Lord your personal King of kings, Lord of lords, and ruler of your heart. If anything else rules your thoughts, such as bitterness, un-forgiveness, addictions, and deceit, then he cannot rule there.

As I have moved into the most recent season of my own life, I rest in the true freedom that is a relationship with Christ. I do not have to always be right` or have things figured out. I do not need to overanalyze the next step. I trust in the Lord. As different areas of my own life need improving, so will yours. I may grab onto bitterness and not let it go. Then, after recognizing it and working through it, I release it. But inevitably, something else creeps up, perhaps anger, or a harsh tongue, but something. We are not perfect. We never will be.

Accept right now that you will never be the absolute perfect mom. Recognize that you will not always say the right things. You will never have the perfect face or perfect body shape, according to what the world's standard portrays. But most importantly, recognize that you are the perfect one to raise your child. God chose you. Recognize that you have the perfect appearance, made just for you, courtesy of your gracious and loving heavenly Father. Accept his mercy and grace. Work hard to be the best you can be in all areas and allow yourself to be forgiven when you fail.

The prayer that I wrote in my journal many years ago and refer to often is as follows.

Search me, Father. Reveal areas in my life that I am not right in. Forgive me. Help me know that every single day is a fresh start. My beginning starts today, right now. It is new. Lord, thank you that your grace is sufficient and that your mercy is new every morning. Give me an excitement for my life. Remind me daily what my purpose is. Give me the grace to walk in that purpose and allow me to forgive myself, just as you have forgiven me. Amen.

Imagine what type of mom you would be if you allowed God to fight your battles. We get caught up in wanting to be right, seeking revenge on those who hurt us, or feeling sorry for what has been done to us. We do not give it to God. I challenge you today to turn it all over to him. Begin to see yourself as a new person, a new creation. Start your life, today. Look at parenting with a new perspective. Respect what God has given you. The Creator of this world has entrusted you with the life of a son or daughter. Be honored. Be free.

WHOM THE SON SETS FREE...
WEEK 11

Describe freedom in your own words.

_____

_____

_____

_____

What is bondage? What are some areas in which you have experienced bondage?

_____

_____

_____

_____

As Christians, we choose to walk in freedom by avoiding sin. It holds us captive. What does Psalm 119:45 say about this?

_____

_____

_____

_____

Consider forgiveness. Is there someone in your life that you need to forgive? Are you withholding forgiveness from yourself in any area? Let go of it today. Decide today that bitterness, un-forgiveness, and shame will not hold you captive.

_____

_____

_____

_____

Has there been a time in your life when it was difficult to accept discipline? How do you think this affects your ability to discipline your children?

_____

_____

_____

_____

Write Proverbs 3:11–12 here.

_____

_____

_____

PRAYER:

Heavenly Father, there are many areas where I have lived in bondage. I have walked through life feeling burdened by my past. Release me of that right now. Allow me to release myself of it. Allow me to be free to accept and give forgiveness. Allow me to accept and give discipline in an appropriate manner. Amen.

WHOM THE SON SETS FREE...
WEEK 12

Do you struggle with the need to always be right? Is it important to you to have others share your opinion? Ask God to reveal to you those areas where you should stand your ground and those where you should resolve to keep quiet.

_____

_____

_____

_____

Do you give every area of your life to the Lord? Do you trust him with your finances, your relationships, and your parenting?

_____

_____

_____

_____

Release yourself right now from any need to be perfect. Allow yourself room to make mistakes and grow. Write a promise to yourself here.

_____

_____

_____

_____

Take the time right now to write a prayer to God. Bear your heart and soul to him on paper.

_____

_____

_____

_____

_____

_____

_____

_____

_____

Make a list of areas in your life in which you are thankful. Refer to it often.

_____

_____

_____

_____

_____

_____

_____

PRAYER:

Thank you, Lord, that I am changed. Thank you for all you have revealed to me through this book and your Word. Continue to change me and grow me. Help me not be who I was. I praise you for your grace and mercy. Amen.